GOOD NUTRITION?

GOOD NUTRITION?

Fact and fashion in dietary advice

Patricia A. Crotty

ALLEN & UNWIN

© Patricia A. Crotty 1995

First published in 1995

Allen & Unwin Pty Ltd
9 Atchison Street, St Leonards, NSW 2065 Australia

National Library of Australia
Cataloguing-in-Publication entry:

Crotty, Pat
  Good nutrition: fact and fashion in dietary advice

  Bibliography.
  Includes index.
  ISBN 1 86373 730 8.

  1. Nutrition—History. 2. Nutrition—Social aspects—History. 3. Diet—
  History. 4. Nutrition—Government policy. I. Title

363.809

Set in 10/11.5 pt Garamond by DOCUPRO, Sydney

Printed by SRM Production Services Sdn Bhd, Malaysia

10 9 8 7 6 5 4 3 2 1

Contents

Preface

A meritorious program has worthy goals, achieves its standards of effectiveness, provides benefits to its participants, fully informs its participants of the potential risk of participation and does no harm. (Fink 1993)

Patricia Crotty's historical study of the development of nutritional science is both timely and controversial. Her book is concerned with the various ways in which scientific ideas and moral values are interrelated and interconnected in dietetics. Its principal thesis is that the development of a scientific discourse of good nutrition, which started in the late nineteenth century and has continued through the twentieth century, either inevitably embraces a moral view of the good life or implicitly provides a vision of a moral order which is disguised by a bogus scientific language. Clearly the second version of the argument will provoke more scientific protest and disquiet. Certainly the question 'Does good nutrition lead to the good life?' is one to which we need a clear and reliable answer. This study will be of particular interest to women and to the elderly, for whom, Crotty argues, current theory about good nutrition, particularly with respect to the relationship between cholesterol and heart disease, has little direct relevance. Crotty also demonstrates the lack of understanding of the everyday world which characterises scientific theories of nutrition and shows that without an adequate sociology of eating, diet and everyday life, promotional campaigns defending one or other variation on the heart disease theme will be relatively unsuccessful or even negative and inappropriate. This study will reinforce a suspicion among the public that nutritional theory is subject to non-rational fads and fashions in science, many of which may have undesirable consequences for the lay population. It thus raises crucial questions about the role of experts and expert systems in modern society, where science has penetrated deep into the organisation and practices of everyday activities such as eating and cooking. Within the framework of an historical study of the complex interrelationship between nutrition theory, dietary practice and moral campaigns—particularly those aimed at changing or reforming working-class dietary practices—this book also asks provocative and important questions about health, diet and public policy. It is to be hoped, therefore, that it will reach the widest possible audience, both within and outside the academy. This book is of critical importance for the reform of public policy on health in contemporary society.

Although my own view of the evidence she presents is positive, my intention here is to locate Crotty's argument within the framework of the sociology of the body in order to reinforce the view that scientific argument is inevitably bound up with moral positions and that the distinction between facts and values is in practice difficult to sustain. I shall approach this issue via a sociological commentary on the notion of diet and rations.

In European thought, the human body has for centuries been a metaphor or theme for the analysis of secular political institutions. Corporeal metaphors were a dominant tool for analysing political behaviour well into the seventeenth century, when the doctrine of individual property rights was more fully and adequately articulated by political theorists such as John Locke. Certainly the analogy between the body and society was particularly important in conceptions of sovereignty such as the medieval theory of kingship. The king was thought to have two bodies: a secular material body which was subject to decay and corruption, and a spiritual body which was symbolic of the continuity of the political community. When on the death of a king his followers shouted 'The king is dead, long live the king,' they were affirming that the death of the king's material body would not impinge upon the continuity of his spiritual body. These ideas about the body politic were drawn from Christian theology, in which the Church was conceptualised as Christ's body and religious institutions were thought to embody the charismatic authority of Christ. The Church as a body was bound together by celebration of the sacraments, particularly the Eucharist, which, as a meal, connected the faithful to the body of Christ.

Communal meals are an essential aspect of human sociability. Moral views of the body were inevitably tied to political visions of major social institutions. The health of the social body was seen to depend upon the individual bodies of its constituent members, while the health of individuals was also a reflection of the general health of the community. Moral practices of individuals were seen to be both reflections of and building blocks for collective well-being.

Medical theory, practice and science have played an important part in these moral views of the body and appropriate conduct. In Greek medicine, diet (*diaita*, or mode of living) referred to the general conduct and organisation of an individual's life, including dress, domestic arrangements, behaviour and attitudes. In classical Greece, diet referred not to a limited or confined set of eating practices but rather to a general outline for life and conduct. Diet was an essential feature of Greek medical regimens, the sets of rules or guidelines imposed upon people to secure their well-being. Regimen also has an archaic meaning of 'government'; it is the root of our words regime and regiment. A political diet in the Holy Roman Empire was a legislative assembly. The *diaita* was a general mode of living which arose from a particular government of the body brought about by medical practices.

If a body well regulated or governed by a medical regimen indicates the presence of discipline, self-control and moral conduct, then of course an obese body indicates the absence of government and discipline. The out-of-control body is a moral challenge to medical government, much as anarchy is a social and moral threat to a well-ordered kingdom. Here again we see corporeal metaphors applied in the analysis of good individual behaviour and good government. Diet continued to be a moral as well as medical regime through the modern period. In the eighteenth century, for example, a well-balanced body was thought to be an essential foundation for a stable mind, and it was common to draw a causal connection between, for example, suicide and poor diet on the basis that, as it was thought, a disordered body was constitutive of a disordered mind. In Scotland in the middle of the eighteenth century, George Cheyne became famous for his dietetic explanations of suicide or the 'English malady'.

This view of the close relationship between moral conduct and the regulation of the body persisted through the nineteenth century in philosophy and political thought. For example, the German social philosopher Ludwig Feuerbach (1804–1872), who was important in the development of materialism and Marxism, was influenced by current nutritional theory and made popular the notion that 'man is what he eats'. Feuerbach took issue with the idea of human beings as simply cognitive beings. He wanted to promote a view of human beings as sensuous, active agents involved in a dynamic relationship between their external environment and the internal environment of their sensations. From this perspective, human beings are the products of their productive activity in that they create themselves through labouring on their conditions of existence, which include the fundamental activities of reproduction and consumption. This view of human sensual activity contributed significantly to Marxist materialism, although the emphasis on the human body was eventually lost in Marx's economic theories.

One might have expected that with the secularisation of Western cultures and the decline of religious institutions, views about diet would also become scientific and secular. One might assume that the ancient moral discourse of the medical diet would be transformed and replaced by a neutral language of nutrition. Certainly there were important changes in scientific theories about nutrition in the nineteenth century. By 1840, German chemists had identified three major chemical constituents of food, namely fats, carbohydrates and proteins, and had begun to calculate the human requirements for each of these components. By the 1880s the scientific laws relating to the conservation of energy were being applied to living organisms. Nutritional scientists began to measure the potential energy in food and the energy which is expended in human labour in terms of calories, the units used in thermodynamics to measure mechanical work. It was typical in the late nineteenth century for scientists to regard food as fuel for the human engine. Nutritional science became an important approach to assessing and improving the effectiveness of human labour. It was applied, through rationing, to institutionalised or captive populations in prisons or in the armed forces. Crotty shows that nutritional science became part of a moral campaign to improve the living conditions of the working class by reducing the cost of food via more efficient means of cooking and eating. She also shows that these nutritional strategies emerged within a context of conflictual labour relations in which nutritional science held out the promise of containing the demand for increased wages by the working class by reducing the cost of eating. Behind the growth of nutritional science lay strong political and moral motives to regulate the working class. It is interesting here to reflect upon the ambiguities of the notion 'to ration'. A ration is an allowance of provisions but it also means, as a verb, to subject to a rationing scheme. It is also associated with the notion of rationalisation, which in everyday terms means the development of planning and regulation. However in sociology rationalisation, following the work of the German sociologist Max Weber, also refers to the growth of science and its application to everyday procedures and activities, the decline of magic and super-stition in everyday life, and finally the imposition of routines, order and process on social institutions and social behaviour. In this respect we can regard the growth of nutritional science in society as a rationalisation of conduct, that is as the imposition of scientific norms and practices on everyday relations, attitudes and activities. Clearly it is much easier within this paradigm to impose a rationalised diet on captive or institutionalised audiences than on the general public. There has, however, been a rationalisation of the industry of eating and consumption through such developments as the McDonald's hamburger chain, which has applied Henry Ford's production theories to the preparation of food to enable standardisa-tion of patterns of consumption throughout the fast food industry. In fact the management principles involved in the 'McDonaldisation' of the food industry can also be applied in universities to law, medicine and journalism, resulting in the 'McDonaldisation of society' (Ritzer 1993).

Returning to the moral meanings of dieting, Crotty clearly indi-cates that, while there has indeed been a scientific transformation of nutritional knowledge and practice, the social policy outcomes of nutritional science still contain an important moral dimension. As she shows, contemporary public health policy is heavily geared toward promoting low-fat diet, despite lingering scientific uncer-tainty about the effectiveness of such a strategy in reducing mor-bidity and mortality rates. A low-fat-diet public health policy is based upon on the idea that there exists, particularly in the male middle-class, an unhealthy stratum of people who are overweight and therefore at risk of illness and early death. These nutritional ideas obviously integrate well with current organisational theory about the importance of a good corporate image. The modern corporation, working in an environment of international uncertainty, has to be lean and mean, and its corporate leaders are expected to have bodies which reflect the ideology of organisational fitness. Obese corporate managers are not only exposed to a health risk, they are a risk to the corporation because their bodies suggest a contradiction between the needs of the corporation as an institution and the public image of corporate leaders. We can see here the persistence of the body as a metaphor of society, but we might also remind ourselves that the very word 'corporation' is derived from the Latin *corpus*, or body. Just as the state of the king's body reflected the health of the political community, so the body of the corporate leader reflects the financial health of the organisation. In a period when public institutions are guided by economic rationalism, it is implicitly believed that a corporation cannot be corpulent.

Contemporary society places enormous emphasis on the human body. The body plays a crucial role in advertising many commodities, for which its shape and image are constantly employed as a sign. This focus on the body is an obvious feature of the fashion and food industries but it extends throughout the whole arena of popular culture. At the same time there is an enormous anxiety about the body which is associated with such issues as the AIDS epidemic, the pollution of the food chain, and the use of medical science in reproduction technologies and transsexual surgery. The problem of ageing bodies has important consequences for social policy and economic growth. The capacity and nature of the body are also being transformed by the development of computer-generated artificial bodies, particularly in techniques of so-called virtual reality. These technical, scientific and social transformations raise fundamental questions about the nature of the body, the boundary between the body and culture, and identity both human and individual. In the world of advanced technology and biomedical sciences, who owns the body?

While technology opens up enormous opportunities for growth and change, these transformations of society and identity also expose us to increased levels of risk. The idea developed by the German sociologist Ulrich Beck that we now live in a 'risk society' (Beck 1991) has taken strong hold in western Europe. Beck argues that modernisation has been accompanied by a fundamental change in the nature of risk. In traditional society, risks were typically observable, local and personal. Interpersonal violence is one example. By contrast, Beck says, modern risks are often unobservable, global, impalpable and impersonal. The hole in the ozone layer is a good example of a modern risk. Environmental damage of this kind resulting from industrialisation produces a generalised risk which is not directly observable by individuals but which influences all of us. In this sense, Beck argues that whereas poverty was hierarchical, smog is democratic. By this rather controversial claim he means that environmental damage puts all human beings at risk regardless of class or location. He believes that as a consequence of changes in the nature of risk the very nature of social solidarity has been transformed. While solidarity in traditional societies was based upon need, the social solidarity of the contemporary world is a solidarity of anxiety. Societies were originally organised to protect their members against lack, and most welfare systems were developed around some notion of need and necessity. These ideas have become institutionalised in such welfare institutions as departments of social security. In the contemporary world, we are more concerned by the insecurities and risks which envelop us all: although contemporary societies often enjoy economic abundance, they are nevertheless bound together psychologically by a common appreciation of the globalisation of risk, hazard and uncertainty. Modern political systems are thus often organised not only to achieve growth but to contain risk, uncertainty and hazard. In Beck's view, the risks of modern society are the unintended but global and inescapable consequences of industrialisation and modernisation.

Beck illustrates his arguments with a variety of specific examples, but his commentary on the effects of instrumental rationalism and science on society is probably best represented by his account of medical science, medical professionalisation and iatrogenic illness. For Beck, modern medical practice is protected from public scrutiny by the development of the clinic, which provides an institutional roof under which research and medical training can be securely interlinked. Within this context, medicine operates in the arena of sub-politics—that is, it can often bypass the formal democratic political structures of modern society, developing its own interests and power base. Medicine within the clinic functions beyond the regulation of law and the state. In addition the speed of medical development and technological change means that the general public is typically presented with the details of a medical problem long after they are relatively well established in experimental medicine. Examples of such *faits accomplis* include the effects of thalidomide on unborn babies, and accidental transmission of viral diseases like mad cow disease and Creutzfeldt-Jakob disease. The food chain may also be threatened by the unintended consequences of microbiology. The health hazards posed by pesticides and asbestos are only now being fully recognised. A further consequence of these changes is that contemporary political debate is often dependent upon the often inconclusive and contradictory evidence of experts, yet which lay audiences are seldom in a position to evaluate properly. For example, governments are often unable to comprehend and analyse the ramifications of such developments as the computerisation of knowledge, scientific advances in agriculture, or technical change in medicine—with obvious consequences for policy. Expert advice may be contradictory or obscure and complicated. Government decisions on such issues cannot, therefore, be in a strict sense rational. The general public, too, is ill-equipped to make sensible judgments about many technological innovations. There is a growing gap between lay belief and practice and scientific knowledge, despite the need for the lay public to be informed, at least in an elementary sense, of the health consequences of, for example, using a particular type of detergent.

These ideas from the sociological debate about the 'risk society' have a clear application to the problems and issues discussed in this excellent book. The general public lacks the training needed to understand the scientific issues which lie behind modern dietetics and its debates about calories, vitamins, protein and so on. Complicated and often contradictory data and findings are reduced to simplistic formulae like 'eat less fat'. Such slogans work very well, however, because they trade upon a set of anxieties about the self and the body which are common in modern societies, particularly among women. In contemporary society, one could argue, we have moved towards a representational self which is highly dependent upon the regard of others. In sociology, this notion of the representational self has been captured by a variety of expressions, perhaps the most apt of which is the 'looking-glass self'. This self is constituted by the reflection of the self in the other. One's sense of importance or value, in other words, is exclusively dependent upon the positive appraisal of significant others. Furthermore, the appraisal of the self is now focused on the *image* of the body. Being good in contemporary society is closely associated with looking good, and looking good has been closely associated with slimness and the regulated lifestyle of an ascetic self. Of course, diet and self-regulation were, for many centuries, part of a religious discipline which aimed to control the soul. In modern society such bodily asceticism is designed to produce an acceptable social self, particularly a self that conveys sexual symbolism. Looking good in our society means looking sexually attractive, and for women this has come to mean being thin. The modern soul or psyche is expressed through the body, that is through a sexually charged body image which is socially good. While nutritional scientists may have produced the slogan 'eat less fat' with the aim of reducing mortality rates in advanced industrial societies, 'eat less fat' is acceptable in popular culture because it is understood within a discourse of the sexual body. It is for this reason that the whole question of diet is inextricably bound up with the problem of modern personal identity. A good body image is important to a good self-image; in a culture in which life expectancy has increased considerably in the past century and in which youthfulness is highly valued, a youthful slim body is a major personal and social asset which must be maintained for a lifetime.

While it is literally the case that 'man is what he eats', this book highlights the fact that in a powerful metaphorical sense, woman is what *she* eats. The dark side of the slimming industry is the evolution of anorexia nervosa as a medical condition primarily affecting women. Anorexia nervosa is a peculiarly valuable metaphor of the modern condition in the sense that it reveals many of the underlying contradictions and problems of contemporary life. While this book is at one level a sustained and important discussion of good nutrition, it raises problems which are fundamental to the notion of the good life in a social context charged with considerable risk and hazard. Understanding good nutrition, therefore, should improve our understanding of good politics.

Bryan S. Turner
Deakin University

1

Introduction

How else but in a framework of magic could we reconcile ourselves to the fact that our continued existence depends on shovelling into ourselves bits of dead animals and things dug out of the ground? (McLaughlin 1978)

If the people set aside to instruct us cannot help, we must do it ourselves. We must do our own balancing, according to what we have learned and also, for a change, according to what we have thought. (Fisher 1976)

I have a conscientious objection to community-wide dietary reform.

I have chosen the term conscientious objection because my criticisms of dietary reform are based not only on the shortcomings of its scientific underpinnings but also on its lack of social perspective and compassion. This book looks at dietary reform which persuades the community at large to change its diet to prevent heart disease, principally by reducing fat consumption. I refer to this reform as 'Good Nutrition'. In my view, rational decisions about Good Nutrition will not be made until its proponents—governments, nutrition scientists, health promoters and dietitians—recognise that community dietary reform is not solely about medical science but equally about values, priorities, vested interests, concepts of morality, and conformity.

Contemporary low-fat dietary reform is, however, only one example of a broader social process with a venerable historical tradition. This process has been studied by sociologists and social historians. Dietary reform as a 'social problem' falls within the purview of sociology. My interest in the area is based mainly on

1

my training as a health practitioner. I am interested in the consequences for the community and for professional practice when Good Nutrition is naively assumed to be 'scientific' and therefore beyond debate.

The object of this book, then, is to encourage wider debate about programs advising the general community to adopt particular eating habits. I cover the process by which the public is given dietary advice based on orthodox medicine; I do not discuss alternative health concepts. I have used the term Good Nutrition because it contains the two key elements of the dilemma I am examining, that is, the relationship between 'cultural' and 'scientific' ideas about food and health. This book argues that, while there is a scientific basis for understanding diet and health, culture drives the way in which dietary advice for the public is developed. It is the combination of science with culture that creates Good Nutrition, and it is the nature of this combination as it exists today that I explore here.

The book will be of interest to those who plan and conduct public information programs about diet and to students of health promotion. I hope it will also be of interest to the wider community, particularly those who feel irritated about restrictive, fallible dietary advice. It suggests ways of understanding how and why dietary advice is developed, maintained and changed.

Those who want clear-cut, authoritative rules to guide their food choices, and experts who want to give advice in this way, will not find satisfaction here. My arguments do not simplify the nature of Good Nutrition; on the contrary, they portray the process of developing healthy eating messages as a complicated one. This is because I believe it is indeed a much more complex process than is generally accepted, particularly by those who give dietary advice.

Although I discuss the late-19th-century beginnings of modern dietary advice, my principal focus is on the changes in Good Nutrition from the postwar period to the heart-disease prevention campaigns of the 1980s.

My three main propositions are that:

- Good Nutrition messages are a mixture of ideas from both science and culture
- This mixture constitutes a form of social control, and
- This control is more restrictive of women than of men.

As a result, I argue, changes should be made in the way dietary advice is developed and disseminated so that the general public can follow, and, where possible, participate in any debates. Through a critical analysis of the current situation, I draw attention to its particular disadvantages for women, and explore some ideas for developing a more participatory and less authoritarian concept of Good Nutrition. In particular, I argue that the cultural component of Good Nutrition should be acknowledged by scientists and that it should incorporate more broadly representative community values.

Basing my critique on the dietary prevention of coronary heart disease, I seek to bring to light the hidden values and beliefs underpinning contemporary community dietary reform. I argue that what could be called the 'contemporary good nutrition project' adds cultural biases to science in ways that can make it moralistic, sexist, and based on class prejudices. I contend that this causes a number of problems, in particular a growing gap between experts' pronouncements and the realities of everyday life, and experts' increasingly irrational use of the available evidence. This is not new; nutrition scientists in the past have often misunderstood the centrality of domestic life to dietary behaviour.

Other writers have tackled some aspects of these problems. Thomas J. Moore's *Heart Failure: A Critical Inquiry into American Medicine and the Revolution in Heart Care* covers a number of issues related to heart disease and includes a chapter on prevention, including diet. *Good Nutrition* differs from *Heart Failure* in that it refers largely to Australia and concentrates on dietary education only, rather than on other aspects of heart disease such as medical care and surgery.

At least two publications of The Social Affairs Unit in London (a conservative policy think tank) cover similar areas. *Who Needs WHO*, published in 1992, is a critique of the WHO dietary guidelines by three authors, all of whom are well-known dissidents in the diet–heart debate and two of whom (Mike Gibney and Petr Skrabanek) I make reference to. *A Diet of Reason: Sense and Nonsense in the Healthy Eating Debate*, edited by Digby Anderson and published in 1986 has a number of chapters written by experts in particular fields, e.g. medicine and agricultural economics, and covers similar but much broader issues mainly from a scientific perspective rather than a social one.

One chapter in *The Politics of Health Education: Raising the Issues* (1986), edited by S. Rodwell and A. Watts, raises concerns about Good Nutrition and education for women in families similar to those expressed here. *Health Scare: The Misuse of Science in Public Health Policy* (1991) by J.R. Johnstone and C. Ulyatt, is a

'Eating Right' choices for Americans, US Department of Agriculture

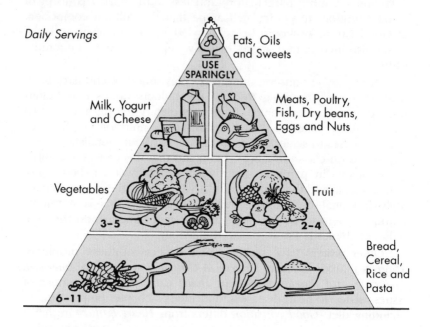

Daily Servings

Fats, Oils and Sweets
USE SPARINGLY

Milk, Yogurt and Cheese
2-3

Meats, Poultry, Fish, Dry beans, Eggs and Nuts
2-3

Vegetables
3-5

Fruit
2-4

Bread, Cereal, Rice and Pasta
6-11

brief monograph looking at very similar issues to this book but from a free-market and freedom-of-the-individual perspective. It covers passive smoking, alcohol consumption and driving as well as 'good nutrition'.

Both the Social Affairs Unit and the Australian Institute of Public Policy, the publisher of *Health Scare*, are politically conservative. Interestingly, despite some trenchant criticisms of health promotion in general, the left has so far found little to criticise in contemporary dietary reform.

Perhaps the best available books on changing ideas about food and nutrition in the United States are Harvey Levenstein's *Revolution at the Table: The Transformation of the American Diet* and *Paradox of Plenty: A Social History of Eating in America*, both of which have been important sources for this book. But Levenstein does not pursue, from the viewpoint of policy and practice, how we might learn from the past and what strategies might be used to improve community education programs.

The question 'To what extent is Good Nutrition about being "good" and to what extent is it about being "scientific"?' is raised here. Historically, eating 'properly' has been a moral issue in our society as in many others. Good Nutrition is tangled up with beliefs about right and wrong, and this is reflected in such common contemporary terms as 'proper nutrition', 'proper diet', and the more American 'eating right'. This tangle manages to entrap other areas of cultural belief and practice, for example those related to gender.

This book gives priority to the often highly charged associations between food and gender. Women's roles have always been linked with food and nurturance, so it is not surprising that when experts advise on Good Nutrition, the advice activates the culture/science tangle and in its wake brings sexist implications. For this reason, and also because expertise and class are inextricably linked, many public health programs, including those focusing on Good Nutrition, are also classist. They start with the assumptions that there is such a thing as a middle-class lifestyle, that this is a desirable way of life from the point of view of health, and that there is a low-income lifestyle which in turn is undesirable in terms of health. One of the important roles of health programs, then, becomes making the low-income lifestyle approximate the middle-class one, especially in regard to health values and behaviours. This is anything but a modern concept.

Because of these processes, there is a growing gap between experts and the community on the issue of Good Nutrition. Experts have overvalued the practical importance of their biological knowledge of nutrition, and a new and largely unrecognised set of problems has been created because nutrition experts have been blind to the historical and cultural nature of their mission. The first six chapters of this book discuss contemporary education about nutrition and its historical origins. The last chapter provides a basis for revising our current ideas of Good Nutrition and proposes that nutrition education and nutrition policies should be based on a better combination of science with social reality. It discusses the possible impact of these ideas on research, policy, and public education programs.

This book argues then, that programs to persuade the community to eat for health are more in need of reform than community dietary habits. It is about the conflict between medical science's view of Good Nutrition and the practicalities of everyday life. It argues for shifting the reforming focus of Good Nutrition away from people's behaviour towards nutrition itself. I have not been very exact in defining 'scientific experts' in this context. I use the term chiefly to refer to those offering opinions on Good Nutrition who are trained in what could be called 'post-swallowing sciences', such as medicine, physiology and biochemistry, rather than in 'pre-swallowing' sciences, such as sociology, psychology and anthropology.

A number of colleagues and friends read and gave valuable comments and criticisms on the difficult early versions of this book. I particularly appreciate the assistance of Dr Diana Elton, Professor Margaret Cameron, Rosemary Stanton and Jan Winstanley. Thanks to Catherine Paton for help with word processing and library sources and Elizabeth Weiss and Jo Jarrah of Allen & Unwin.

2

Giving advice

The biology of nutrition is complex, but its application in everyday life must be practical and simple. For example, to be effective, diet reform efforts need to recognise that culture, not biology, constructs everyday life. While it may be true that biological needs drive life—we must all breathe, eat, drink, sleep and excrete—our knowledge of those needs and the way we use that knowledge are founded in culture. This book distinguishes between what human bodies do with food and the use to which we put our knowledge of that process.

We must eat certain nutrients to live, but biology plays only a limited role in food choice. There are only plants and animals and their products to eat, yet all societies and individuals limit their selection of both. Nutrition advice and education, however, are only a small part of the broad and complex basis for food choices—and the behavioural change and health outcomes they produce are ultimately little more than fine-tuning.

To more completely understand the debate about diet and the prevention of coronary heart disease, and the relationship between that debate and Good Nutrition, we need a new perspective. After a 30-year history of research and practice, there is still uncertainty and some disagreement in the medical literature on this important health issue. Researchers from a variety of backgrounds have looked at the existing data on diet and heart disease and come up with a variety of interpretations. In particular there are different views about what social action should be taken in light of the research findings. Some believe whole nations should be persuaded to change their diets. Others looking at the same findings believe that such programs are not warranted by the available evidence. Some epidemiologists, for example, have stated that the well-known Finnish community intervention program the North Karelia Project reduced heart disease and disability. Other experts (including a member of the team who conducted that project) have disagreed (Salonen 1987). This uncertainty is rarely reflected in community education programs. Among those who support national dietary reform, however, there is remarkable agreement. Geoffrey Cannon, a British writer and outspoken supporter of dietary reform, has pointed out the strong international consensus on Good Nutrition among experts and governments (Cannon 1991). But as is discussed in Chapter 7, the fact that a viewpoint is held by a majority of experts is no guarantee that it is right. Nutrition experts reaching a consensus is rather like the guardians of Australian Rules football saying they all agree on the rules of their game. It may be entirely appropriate that the Australian Rules experts agree on the rules of their game, but theirs is not the only game in town. Many people play cricket or basketball. Moreover, a friendly family game of non-experts may look very different from the game that the experts agree upon. Nor should we accept without question that Australian Rules is the best game of all, or even the best it could be. This raises questions about whose opinion matters in the debate. Is it possible for people who are not nutrition experts to develop their own point of view on the social action recommended by nutrition scientists?

The diet–heart debate is carried on mainly by experts in medical research—and in their own terms. Joining the debate is difficult, even for someone trained as a health practitioner such as a dietitian, and joining a debate is different from being heard in it. In all debates some views are valued more highly than others. Health practitioners are rarely as knowledgeable about the intricacies of, say, blood lipids as researchers are, and it would be professionally reckless (and presumptuous) to debate the details of current lipid research with such an expert. Nevertheless, it is often researchers, epidemiologists, nutritionists or medical specialists who express their opinion as to what constitutes Good Nutrition and advise the government or community on what people's food choices should be. Their own expertise may not include health education, cooking for a family, behavioural science, or social policy.

One result of the nutrition science experts' ability to control the grounds of the debate is that practitioners may not be independent enough to control the terms of their own practice. For example, there is currently very little debate among dietitians and health educators about problems associated with low-fat diets for women and children.

My argument for wider participation in decisions on Good Nutrition is based on a view of Good Nutrition as a partially cultural enterprise that should be open to input from the community at large. Just as the community has, through various institutions, come to have a say on highly technical scientific issues such as in-vitro fertilisation and euthanasia, community interests and values should also influence the Good Nutrition debate.

If Good Nutrition is partly a cultural issue, members of the community have an obvious role to play in commenting on their experiences of Good Nutrition, whether in their capacity as the targets of public education or as parents trying to make use of Good Nutrition messages in provisioning and running a domestic kitchen.

Appropriate roles, together with the limitations of 'knowledge experts' in policy making and priority setting, should be open for wider community discussion; this is further explored in Chapter 7.

Why is it important to question the current situation? One sign that all is not well with contemporary Good Nutrition is that it may not meet the challenge of practicality. Studies of dietitians in Britain have shown that the diets of only a small proportion fulfil the recommendations of national guidelines based on diet–heart concerns. Even after receiving additional advice from study organisers, only a small proportion of the dietitians with the problem diets achieved all the recommendations (Black 1984; Coles-Hamilton *et al.* 1986). Furthermore, many diets which do meet the guidelines for fat consumption are high in sugar (Gibney 1990:250). This may indicate that current dietary recommendations are only a form of nutritional mathematics, giving the various dietary components a greater or lesser share of the total kilojoule intake. If someone changes their diet so that less of its total energy comes from fat, it will derive proportionately more energy from another source, usually carbohydrate. This raises the question of where the problem lies—in the individual's food choices or in contemporary Good Nutrition messages.

After all the niceties of the technical diet-composition debates, we are still left asking: Does the teaching of dietary guidelines, particularly lowering the fat content of a diet, lead to predictable or desirable changes in either food choice or health outcomes?

It would have been possible to enquire into some of these

9

dilemmas from a strictly scientific perspective by reviewing the medical literature and coming to some conclusion about the best dietary advice based on current knowledge. However, this approach has limitations. Focusing a critique of Good Nutrition on the medical literature may be the equivalent of trying to push the bus you're riding in. What if the problems lie in the cultural component of Good Nutrition?

I maintain that the growing gap between Good Nutrition based on 'the latest research findings' and ordinary people's everyday life experiences is due to Good Nutrition's acceptance of the 'naturalistic fallacy'. This is a basic confusion between what is and what 'ought to be'. Kendler (1993) has argued for psychology, that empirical data can inform but not create policy; policy cannot be deduced from facts. Even if there were unequivocal evidence that low-fat diets reduce the prevalence of coronary heart disease, it does not logically follow that low-fat diets are the best kind of diets; that is a value judgment. The superiority or otherwise of a diet has dimensions other than its ability to prevent chronic disease. Nutrition policy debates, therefore, should not be solely the province of nutrition experts.

Since heart disease research is the driving force behind contemporary ideas about Good Nutrition, the main debate has been between medical researchers and epidemiologists most of whom have medical training and all of whom work within the medical or disease-based model. Discussion has focused on whether the available evidence warrants persuading whole populations to change their eating behaviour. This has led the proponents of Good Nutrition to see implementing dietary reform programs as their mission, even though the efficacy of such programs is by no means certain (e.g. Miller & Stephenson 1985:743).

It is clear that action to bring about Good Nutrition is taken in the face of uncertainty. It is a policy choice made to address a social problem, as distinct from a self-evident, factual answer to a scientific problem. This applies to all policy decisions and in that sense is unremarkable. What is important in understanding Good Nutrition as a cultural and political issue, however, is the willingness of dietary change advocates to entertain social control strategies as an appropriate means to their end.

This is how some leading scientists envisage action on food choice flowing from medical research.

> Once a social norm of behaviour has become accepted and (as in the case of diet) once the supply industries have adapted themselves to

10

the new pattern, then the maintenance of that situation no longer requires effort from individuals. The health education phase aimed at changing individuals is, we hope, a temporary necessity, pending changes in the norms of what is socially acceptable. (Rose 1985:37)

Using social control as a lever is even more explicitly countenanced by some obesity researchers:

> The ultimate social pressure treatment would be to increase the social sanctions against obesity, so that being overweight would be a tremendously shameful thing. In this manner obesity would be under external social control, as are other behaviors for which society has learned that internal control is not enough for some as in the case of sexual or criminal acts. (Foreyt *et al.* 1981:159)

In expressing such opinions, these scientists have moved a long way from their laboratories and from epidemiological statistics.

The focus of this critique, then, is not on an analysis in medical terms of the medical arguments (what level of blood cholesterol is important, or how much fat in the diet produces what health effects) but rather on examining why this particular ethos of dietary change has been so widely accepted and why it has been applied to everyone, men, women and children, with so little critical discussion. I believe it is more important in understanding contemporary Good Nutrition to ask the political question of why low-fat dietary reform has won relatively unquestioning approval from experts in Australia and, further, whether medically oriented researchers are the most appropriate group to decide how or if their research should be part of a social-action agenda.

A feminist perspective is particularly potent in revealing the political and cultural nature of Good Nutrition—something to which medical and epidemiological approaches are blind—and can also provide clues to why this gap between the givers and receivers of Good Nutrition advice has developed and continues to widen.

In most writing about Good Nutrition, particularly in the past decade, women's interests are hidden and their opinions and experiences ignored or excluded. Because food is central to women's traditional roles, this perhaps is surprising. In an area of everyday life so central to women's roles and responsibilities, defining what is good, right and healthy has become the province of epidemiologists, doctors, health educators, food manufacturers, television and magazines and, most interestingly of all, dietitians. (Almost 95 per cent of dietitians in Australia are women.) Through this coalition, food has been made a central constituent of what the anthropologist

11

Mary Douglas calls the 'danger messages' in this and other Western countries.

Not all advocates of popular dietary reform are as unaware and unfeeling as those I have just quoted, but these extreme views illustrate the difficulty that many medically oriented experts have in coming to terms with the realities of everyday life—particularly those realities faced by people different from themselves, especially women and working-class people. For these reasons, approaching a critique of Good Nutrition from outside the medical model seems essential.

The gap between the understanding of Good Nutrition held by the experts and that held by the general public is due partly to the increasingly esoteric nature of nutrition knowledge and partly to a lack of understanding about the implications of applying this knowledge. Where once there was blood cholesterol, now there are many fractions and subfractions of blood lipids, each with its own implications for heart disease. Some forms of blood cholesterol are associated with higher risk for heart disease; other types are associated with a protective influence. Fats in food, too, are divided and subdivided into types, each with its own implications for blood fat levels. How this will make advice on Good Nutrition more helpful to consumers is a moot point. Will they be encouraged to scan the label and discover the fatty-acid composition of a food before buying it? Becoming a combination of nutritionist and food chemist does not seem to be a reasonable prerequisite for feeding oneself and one's family. Family food provisioning is much more than biochemistry. We seem to have managed fairly well in the recent past without such complexities, which seem neither an elegant nor a very clever solution to living in the late twentieth century. Rather than making consumers into nutrition experts, perhaps we should put nutrition experts in touch with the realities of food and eating and their place in everyday life.

Experts who develop the scientific knowledge which forms the rationale for community advice are seldom familiar with the social sciences or with the insights they offer into everyday life. Making choices about food in the supermarket is probably an unfamiliar experience to many of those who speak most confidently about what lay people should do.

These same experts may lack an appreciation of how power is exercised in the name of Good Nutrition. Perhaps it would be more accurate to say that they appreciate how to use this power but are unaware of its impact. The British nutritionist John Rivers in 1979 branded the dispassionate objectivity of scientists as a myth. Scientists not only pursue truth but also seek research grants and professional success. Although many people are killed by malnutrition, he noted, many scientists are 'kept alive' by it (Rivers 1979). Rivers was referring to undernutrition in developing countries, but his comment is equally applicable to 'malnutrition' as it is understood in the developed countries.

How does a medical or nutrition practitioner or a member of the community make use of experts' views when the experts themselves are uncertain about the meaning of the available data? And what can 'ordinary' people do when the complexity of science is an impediment to developing their own views on how they should eat? Randall Albury believes that the common image of science as dealing in unquestionable truths obstructs the critical assessment of science and its applications by the general public and scientists alike (Albury 1983:52). This is an important issue for contemporary Good Nutrition. If nutrition is to be part of the World Health Organization's Primary Health Care movement, which encourages community participation in health planning and programs, the development of Good Nutrition messages and programs must become a more inclusive process. But how can non-experts participate in a discussion from which they are excluded because medical expertise has taken over the arena? Is it possible to halt the widening of the gap between Good Nutrition and everyday life, between experts and the community?

While the first six chapters of this book offer a long list of problems many of which are not widely recognised by nutrition knowledge experts, the last chapter looks at a possible way of thinking about these ideas and suggests some strategies which might enable the community to exert greater influence on experts and on the shape of Good Nutrition programs.

In developing a critique of Good Nutrition, it is important to take account of the fact that other critiques are possible from other perspectives. For example, The Australian Institute for Public Policy (AIPP), whose stated aim is to 'encourage understanding and appreciation of the free society and free enterprise', has produced, in *Health Scare* (Johnstone & Ulyatt 1991), a critique of the uses of science to underpin public health policy which shares some criticisms with this book. The authors discuss the orthodoxy surrounding some views of public health and health promotion and the discouraging of dissent from those views, the biased nature of some interpretations of research and their use to justify policy, and the

13

pressures applied to the community to change its behaviour for uncertain benefit. The values behind *Health Scare* and this book differ markedly in at least two respects. Although Johnstone and Ulyatt recognise that the diet–heart debate virtually ignores women as research subjects, it offers anything but a feminist critique of this—indeed the essay by Ulyatt, while expressing concern about the 'paternalistic' nature of state 'interference' in the lifestyle of its citizens, persists in using the (female) gender-linked terms 'nanny state' and 'nannyism', to refer to the offending government and bureaucratic structure and attitude.

Also, while they criticise the role of professional, government, private and bureaucratic interests and the emotional manipulation that often characterises health messages in advertising and the mass media, Johnstone and Ulyatt ignore the private sector's role in broadcasting and magnifying the effect of dietary (and other) reforms. Yet the grand prize for hypocrisy in diet reform messages clearly goes to the private sector. Companies have no compunctions about advertising the health benefits of their high-fibre products while continuing to promote their high-sugar products—even though the 'expert' consensus only supports the former. This opportunistic use of health messages when they help sales, and the studied ignoring of these same messages when they do not, should be a cause for considerable dismay.

In Victoria in February 1992, the producer of a range of low-fat dairy products was promoting full-fat products using a 'nanny state' theme along the lines: 'recently they've told us what to do and what to think . . . even what to eat . . . and they haven't always been right'. The advertisement went on to use a 'freedom' theme to promote the full-fat product. The free market is capable of a degree of hypocrisy in the use of public health arguments that the so-called nanny state could never get away with.

What follows is underpinned by a sense of frustration that Good Nutrition programs are more likely to serve the interests of those with the most knowledge and the greatest control of resources. Raising these issues for wider debate will, I hope, lead to a more equitable distribution of the benefits of our understanding of the relationship between food and health in the context of everyday life. This book does not offer dietary advice but rather a way of understanding how dietary advice is developed—and how community as well as expert interests might be represented in that process.

3

Dietary guidance: history, rationale and a critique

Dietary advice can be seen as a cultural product. Good Nutrition represents contemporary food wisdom, and more than one version of contemporary wisdom can exist. The history of dietary guidance from the time it was first claimed to be based on modern science clearly illustrates this process. If contemporary dietary guidelines are a particular form of Good Nutrition, whose wisdom do they represent and how did they become the dominant Good Nutrition paradigm? What factors led to such guidelines becoming the public face of Good Nutrition in Western nations in the 1970s and 1980s? The central discussion here is a historical account of the cultural uses of science in the name of Good Nutrition. The career of Wilbur Olin Atwater in the late nineteenth and early twentieth century illustrates a number of aspects of my critique: class prejudice, social control and the entrepreneurial uses by nutrition scientists of the social application of their knowledge.

Atwater was probably the first dietary reformer to appeal to laboratory science for the justification of his social action programs. However, his programs were biased against the poor and working classes of the time and designed to serve the interests of the newly emerging industrial economy in the United States. This raises the question of how we evaluate social reforms which appeal to science or formal knowledge for their justification. Do we have to be experts in science and nutrition to participate in the discussion? Where nutrition knowledge is applied to population dietary reform, questions of values and ethics are central. People who are not science

Edward Atkinson   **Ellen Richards**   **W. O. Atwater**
                         (Swallow)

experts can and should have an equal say with scientists in the values informing policies and programs.

The first efforts to advise the general public about what to eat on the basis of laboratory science took place in the US in the 1880s. These versions of Good Nutrition are associated with three people in particular. Atwater, a chemist, analysed foods to determine their composition, conducted household food-consumption surveys and measured energy expenditure in both humans and animals. As well as making recommendations about the protein and energy requirements of humans and developing food-composition tables, Atwater sought wide recognition for his work by promoting its relevance to contemporary social problems. His campaign won him financial support from both government and philanthropic groups and individuals. Atwater's supporters included Ellen Swallow Richards, who was also trained in chemistry but did not pursue a career in academic research as this was regarded as an unsuitable occupation for women. Nevertheless, she made a considerable contribution to the development of environmental health as a public health chemist; a chemistry teacher, particularly of young women; and a founder of the home economics movement in the US (Rosen 1974; Vincenti 1987). The third member of the trio was Edward Atkinson, a politically influential industrialist interested in labour relations.

The project these three undertook was to reform working-class eating habits in line with Atwater's research on food composition and the recommended levels of protein and energy in workers' diets. However, the application of their knowledge came with some hefty ideological baggage and in the end influenced the middle class

16

much more than the less affluent. The social historian Harvey Levenstein credits this combination with laying the foundation of important changes in the diet of the American middle class through what he calls the 'New Nutrition' (Levenstein 1988).

Atwater's best known work was conducted while the US was experiencing industrial unrest and societal upheaval. The industrial revolution had changed the face of cities and working and living conditions for workers in the emerging industrial economies. As workers struggled to improve their working conditions and standard of living, civil strife, including strikes and riots, became part of the industrial scene. Atwater saw a connection between his laboratory work and this social conflict.

The sociologist Naomi Aronson (1982a) has suggested that some pressure from Atwater's then employer, Wesleyan University, was at least partly responsible for motivating him to link his work with this social upheaval. Officials of the Methodist university criticised Atwater's work as insufficiently 'philosophical' and as not upholding Christian ideals. Atwater, possibly prompted by this criticism, linked his work with the concept of an appropriate diet for workers. He emphasised the necessity of adequate protein and energy for a productive workforce and promoted the need for workers to learn to follow his nutritional recommendations while not exceeding their budgets. This meant buying cheap cuts of meat and inexpensive carbohydrate-rich foods and limiting consumption of vegetables and fruits.

The Good Nutrition programs resulting from Atwater's work were flawed in two main ways. First, they neglected the importance of vitamins and minerals (which had not yet been discovered), and second, they regarded the enjoyment of food as a privilege of the more affluent—a luxury that the poor could not afford. As a result, these programs, and the practices they encouraged, were inimical to workers' food culture and, potentially, to their health.

The extent to which Atwater's personal beliefs were mixed with his professional interests is indicated by this extract from one of his series of papers for *Century Illustrated*, a monthly magazine which discussed social and technical advances for an educated lay audience. Here Atwater is discussing the problem of waste:

> Things cannot always go on thus. International competition is becoming sharper, our population denser, and the virgin fertility of our soil gradually exhausted. We must reform or retrograde. Unless we mend our ways the future will bring loss instead of gain in material prosperity, and fearful falling away rather than improvement in our morals.

17

The remedy for the evil, so far as it applies to the chief item of our living expenses, our food, must be sought in two things—popular understanding of the elementary facts regarding food and nutrition, and the acceptance of the doctrine that economy is respectable. Here, I believe, is an opportunity for a two-fold propagandism of incalculable usefulness.

A very large body of people in this country say practically, though not in words, for such principles are not formulated by those who follow them: 'To economise closely is beneath us. We do not wish to live cheaply; we want to live well.'

The true Anti-poverty Society is the Society of 'Toil, Thrift and Temperance'. One of the articles of its constitution demands that the principles of intelligent economy shall be learned by patient study and followed in daily life. Of the many worthy ways in which the charity we shall call Christian is being exercised none seems to me more worthy of that appellation than the movement in industrial education, of which teaching the daughters of working-people how to do housework and how to select food and cook it forms a part.

If Christianity is to defend society against socialism must it not make such homely, non-theological teachings as these part of its gospel? If the old dispensation with its sombre doctrine makes the earning of man's bread in the sweat of his face part of the primeval curse, does not the newer dispensation of religion and science make the gaining of support by earnest toil, and the economizing of resources by careful study, a substantial joy of life? (Atwater 1888:445)

Atwater speaks with authority drawn from his technical knowledge but wraps that knowledge in a thick coat of socio-religious values.

Barbara Ehrenreich and Deirdre English have commented that around this time in the development of science there was a shift away from science's earlier role of attacking entrenched authorities. From being a 'revolutionary force opposed to prejudice, folly and obfuscation wherever they arose', scientists came to see their mission, particularly in relation to domestic issues of significance to women, as not so much to seek 'truth', but to pronounce on what was appropriate (Ehrenreich & English 1978:26).

These attitudes, combined with the limited scientific knowledge of the times, led to some exceedingly poor advice for impoverished and low-paid workers in the US. As a result of his concentration on protein and energy, Atwater regarded the consumption by the poor of fruit and vegetables (which are low in both) as a 'conceit' and an inefficient choice. Fruit and vegetables did not rate highly in his 'food energy–muscle work' conceptualisation of nutrition for workers. Similarly, he encouraged the consumption of more white flour

18

and fewer potatoes because flour was a cheaper source of energy (Levenstein 1988:57). This would not be recognised today as a nutritionally equivalent exchange: we now know that potatoes can make an important contribution to vitamin C consumption, particularly in diets lacking fruits and vegetables. Also, potatoes eaten with their skins on contain more fibre than white flour.

Atwater's 1885 dietary survey of factory workers led him to make suggestions on minimum daily protein and calorie requirements; he came to the conclusion that existing wages were adequate if workers learned to eat 'scientifically'. The next year, he claimed that nutrition research could solve labour problems. He based this assertion on his beliefs that nutrition was a science of work (because of the relationship between food energy and muscle power) and that social adjustments should be based on scientific knowledge.

It was known at this time that workers spent between 50 and 60 per cent of their income on food. Atwater and others believed that if workers based their food choices on scientific principles they could save money, which would enable them to improve the quality of other aspects of their lives such as housing. A social program to educate poor and low-paid workers would therefore, they asserted, reduce social tension and improve workers' lives without any need for wealth redistribution. Profits could stay where they belonged, in the hands of the rich. Thus, the Good Nutrition of the day linked dietary recommendations to income. The poorest people were advised to limit their choices to the cheapest types of food consistent with physiological needs (which were thought to comprise only protein and energy). While a greater quantity of food was recommended for manual than for sedentary workers, food was seen as having a definite utilitarian function for the poor, whereas more affluent people were able to choose foods they enjoyed. The middle and upper classes did not entirely escape the ramifications of contemporary Good Nutrition messages, however. Overindulgence was frowned on, partly because it was seen as a bad example to the working class (Aronson 1982b:53).

> [Atwater] believed [his] principles could be applied to economic behaviour, both production and consumption, to solve the wage problem within the existing class structure and without decreasing the profits of capital. Optimal nutrition would increase productivity, thereby increasing the total social wealth to be divided between the classes. At the same time, the application of sound nutritional principles would reduce worker expenditures for food, thereby effectively increasing the buying power of existing wages. (Aronson 1982a:478)

This passage highlights an important influence on many researchers in their struggles to gain support for their work. Aronson uses Atwater's career to illustrate how nutrition has been constructed as a social problem through entrepreneurial activities. In his case, these centred on his claims that nutrition could solve the problems of labour unrest. But such activities had wider ramifications. Aronson notes that nutritionists' interpretation of nutrition problems provided a justification for low wages while at the same time offering advice and ideas that were of little practical use. Contrary to the reformers' claims, their science was not capable of providing a better life for poor and low-paid workers. Aronson accuses nutritionists of the period of applying their knowledge in a 'class-stratified' way. There were foods for the poor and other foods for the more affluent (Aronson 1982a:483).

It is important to recognise that the pressure on the less affluent sections of society did not go unresisted. Aronson quotes Eugene Debs, a Boston labour leader, objecting to 'nutrition advocates' who advised working people to buy cheaper beef and observing, 'nothing is too good for us' (Aronson 1982a:483). Levenstein discusses the animosity between Debs and Atwater's colleague Atkinson. Speaking in relation to Atkinson's campaigning, Debs remarked that American working men would not be further degraded, 'scientifically or otherwise' (Levenstein 1988:56). These early social applications transformed the science of nutrition into Good Nutrition through the missionary activity directed by one social class at another. The advocates of the Good Nutrition model of the time have been described as going about

> their mission among the working class with a smug assurance that with 'science' on their side, they were touting a way of life far superior to that worked out by millions of people in their daily struggle to survive. (Levenstein 1988:55)

One of the harshest assessments of Atwater's contribution to the social application of nutrition principles comes from Hillel Schwartz. Referring to Atwater as the 'son of a Temperance minister' (Schwartz 1986:887), Schwartz charges him with changing the meaning of food by stripping from it all reference to taste, ethnic tradition and social context (Schwartz 1986:887–888). In Atwater's food composition tables, food was reduced to no more than calories and grams of protein, carbohydrate, fat and water.

Atwater's commitment to dietary reform faded as his work on metabolism won government recognition and funding. He was able to acquire the latest technology, an expensive calorimeter in which people could live and have their energy expenditure measured for extended periods. Atwater's interests subsequently moved away from social action to more academic questions.

Schwartz's unrelentingly critical assessment echoes the comments of other observers of this period. During the Second World War, Brigadier Sir Cedric Stanton Hicks, the pioneer of Australian armed-forces catering, visited the US to try to reduce American demand for Australian meat. The eminent nutritionist E. V. McCollum, then a 'grand old man of Nutritional Science', told Stanton Hicks how years before he had taken a younger colleague to a meeting of the American Chemical Society, at which Atwater had presented a famous paper on his food analysis program. At the end of the lecture, the younger scientist asked Atwater whether he had thought of applying such analyses to coal, because the analytic methods were equally applicable; if so, would Atwater therefore call coal a food? What the young scientist was implying, said McCollum, was that food was more than its nutrient constituents (Stanton Hicks 1972:188).

McCollum's contribution to the application of laboratory-gained knowledge offers some counterpoint to Atwater's legacy. A chemist, he was responsible for the discovery of vitamins A and D. His biographer, H. G. Day, refers to him as a scientist-reformer and, dubiously, claims for him the title of instigator of 'popular nutrition education', which dates from about 1915.

McCollum seems to have been less zealous than Atwater in his approach to the reform of Americans' eating patterns. He made a point of speaking out against over-optimism in claiming benefits for Good Nutrition. Day portrays McCollum as moderate and realistic, and says his main piece of advice was 'Use a suitable variety of foods.' This maxim was one of the first tenets of modern scientific nutrition.

In contrast to Atwater's classist and entrepreneurial reform agenda, McCollum's chief interest seems to have lain in promoting public understanding of the new knowledge coming from laboratory work. The moral values underpinning his ideas appear less rigid than Atwater's, for example his 'liberal rule': 'Eat what you want after you have eaten what you should' (Day 1987:38).

However, McCollum seems not to have escaped the belief commonly held by nutrition experts that they are writing on blank slates when they speak to women about food and health. Day records this extract from McCollum's autobiography:

Hitherto women had never heard of such comments on individual foods and combinations of them, nor did they know of the great contrasts in the appearance of animals which the system of feeding could effect.(Day 1987:33)

Levenstein has some harsher words for McCollum, particularly for his incorrect idea that it was important to balance acid-forming and alkali-forming foods in the diet (Levenstein 1988:153).

The work of McCollum and his colleagues was of more interest to processed-food producers than philanthropists. The source of support for nutrition research in the US gradually shifted from philanthropists and governments to corporate sources. McCollum acted as a consultant to a flour milling company and defended the value of white flour against those who had used the new knowledge to condemn it as nutritionally worthless. When vitamins and their dietary significance were being discovered, the corporate sector was developing rapidly and competition among food companies was increasing. It is unclear to what extent McCollum, like Atwater 20 years earlier, was able to use entrepreneurial strategies to support his research.

SCIENCE-BASED GOOD NUTRITION:
THE AUSTRALIAN EXPERIENCE

There are both similarities and important differences between the roles Good Nutrition has played in workers' lives in the US and Australia. Walker and Roberts have chronicled the use of Atwater's data and that of his European and British counterparts in establishing, through legislation, the concept of the 'living wage' for workers (Walker & Roberts 1988).

In the first decade of this century, workers' needs were considered more favourably in Australia than in most other countries, presumably because of the strength of organised labour. This is reflected in Australian discussions relating the new scientific nutrition knowledge to social action. Nevertheless, the sorts of classist attitudes held by Atwater and his contemporaries were also present in Australia—and from an even earlier stage than Atwater's era.

In the early eighteenth century, long before Atwater was born, the new Australian colonies were struggling for survival, and convict labour was central to many government concerns. As Walker and Roberts describe it, the attitude of colonial administrators to rations for convicts bore marked similarities to Atwater's thoughts about food for workers a century later. The food should be sufficient for a person engaged in hard labour, but it should cost as little as possible and should not 'make eating a pleasure' (Walker & Roberts 1988:4).

Towards the end of the 1870s, workers in public health organised themselves into the Australian Health Society and the New South Wales Health Society. Even at this embryonic stage in public health in Australia, Walker and Roberts note the conflation of the latest ideas in medicine with a middle-class reforming push centred on teaching the working class better habits (Walker & Roberts 1988: 46). They cite a story from the magazine of the early public health movement which illustrates contemporary ideas about male drinking behaviour. It was believed that women could control their men's drinking, and the squandering of food money on alcohol, by creating a home environment which was pleasant enough to keep the men indoors. The story tells of one Mrs Maguire, who cleaned up the children and the house so nicely that her husband stayed at home after his tea instead of 'rolling out to the pub' (Walker & Roberts 1988:46).

The law in Australia at this time seems to have been less judgmental than the public health movement. In 1907 the historic decision of Justice Higgins established the principle of the 'living wage', whose normative underpinning included the requirement that it should support 'frugal comfort' for a family of five: two adults and three children (Walker & Roberts 1988:62).

It was estimated that 58 per cent of the average wage was spent on food. Later determinations by the states recognised that the diet supported by the fixed wage should 'correspond to existing food habits'—as distinct from the reformist recommendations of the 'New Nutrition' in the US. Women testified at the wage fixation hearings to their difficulties in purchasing food to their own and their families' satisfaction, and gave details of what the families ate.

Medical evidence on nutrition given in later wage cases included exaggerated estimates of desirable energy and protein intakes—in some cases even higher than Atwater's. The union movement, which called the medical witnesses, no doubt saw the advocacy of greater-than-normal nutritional needs as conducive to more generous wage judgments. In the 1920 wage case Justice Piddington criticised the medical evidence and, as a standard, preferred Atwater's (lower) recommended energy intake to the higher European figures. This apparently led to public exchanges between the lawyers and doctors in which 'the wig got the better of the scalpel' (Walker & Roberts 1988:66).

Sir Cedric Stanton Hicks, a doctor, noted that the 1911 Act aimed to establish a 'healthy, happy, efficient and contented populace' by constructing the basic wage on a dietary scale and that the Piddington decision and subsequent basic wage determinations failed to apply the 1911 principles correctly (Stanton Hicks 1972:26).

According to Walker and Roberts, by 1936, some in Australian organised medicine had adopted a more familiar stance. Commenting on the reports of the Advisory Council on Nutrition, the *Medical Journal of Australia* expressed the opinion that good nutrition could be satisfactorily achieved, people could be better informed about nutrition, and food could be distributed at a lower cost 'without any great economic upheaval' (Walker & Roberts 1988:106). The authors suggest that perhaps 'economic upheaval' was a term obscuring fear of socialism. Atwater too, saw his work in dietary reform as a bastion against socialism, although in his case it was specifically tied to Christianity (Atwater 1888:445).

Other points of view were also presented in the *MJA*, including that the problem of malnutrition was a social issue of maldistribution of income and that poverty, not ignorance was the problem (Walker & Roberts 1988:106).

Science's first foray into Good Nutrition, then, was not always laudable, but it did take a pattern that has become almost a paradigm. The first 'scientific' nutrition educators began as missionaries to the poor and the working class (in part to serve their own interests), and became instead missionaries to the middle class. When it became obvious that they had failed at reforming the poor, Ellen Richards and her colleagues in the American home economics movement turned their attention to the middle class, and Atwater retreated to his laboratory. Levenstein quotes Richards as saying, after the collapse of one project directed at reforming poor and immigrant people's eating habits, that she believed it was the more affluent classes—not the poor—that were in need of 'missionary' work on their diet (Levenstein 1988:88).

Our view so far has been mainly through the eyes of sociologists (Aronson, Ehrenreich and English) and social historians (Levenstein and Schwartz). In trying to assess Atwater and his colleagues' contribution to the birth of a science-based Good Nutrition, it is worth reflecting on a discussion of his work by a modern nutritionist. The widely respected Dr Elsie Widdowson, now in her 80s, has been working in the field of nutrition in Britain since the 1930s. Much of her early work, like Atwater's, involved analysing foods and compiling nutrient composition tables. In a 1986 lecture celebrating Atwater's contribution to nutrition, Widdowson mentioned the social ramifications of his dietary reform activities only once. Referring to Atwater's household food consumption surveys, she noted that their results increased both public and government interest in nutrition and led to increased government support for nutrition research (Widdowson 1987:902). Recently the *Journal of Nutrition* devoted a complete supplement to the proceedings of the W.O. Atwater Centennial Celebration Symposium. The only critical discussion of the social context of Atwater's Good Nutrition activities is in the W.O. Atwater Centennial Memorial Lecture. Kenneth Carpenter remarks that although the sociologist Naomi Aronson has suggested poor people's interests could have been prejudiced through Atwater's work, Atwater himself would not have known this was the case—surely a confirmation of the social blinkers of nutrition scientists. Carpenter then blames Atkinson for knowingly trying to limit workers' wages (Carpenter 1994:1711S).

Perhaps this tells us something about the way knowledge of nutrition is transmitted through medical-scientific channels. One may learn about the science of nutrition but not about the social consequences of its application. This has important implications for the education of scientists who need to understand nutrition, particularly those who are, or who may become, scientist-reformers.

Paradoxically, Elsie Widdowson published in *The Lancet* in 1951 a most extraordinary and interesting example of the interaction of nutritional science with its social context. The paper looks at a group of children in orphanages in postwar Germany, and documents the ill effects on their physical development of the institution's strict, unsympathetic and inconsistent discipline— despite the fact that, during the study, the children were given extra food.

It may be useful to examine some of the practical strategies through which the New Nutrition campaign's rhetoric was realised.

THE ALADDIN OVEN

Two particular projects of the scientific dietary reformers were the development of 'take-out' community food services and the Aladdin oven. Edward Atkinson invented the oven in the late 1880s and marketed it as slow cooking, energy efficient and inexpensive, with both household and commercial applications. The project was

The Aladdin oven

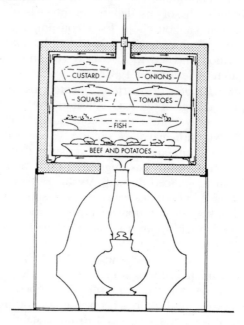

linked with the spread of the New England Kitchens (the original kitchen was established in Boston, Massachusetts, in 1890). These served a hot midday meal intended to provide nourishing, inexpensive food and set a good example to poor and working-class people.

Atkinson developed the stove because he thought workers' wives were inefficient cooks and meal planners. He regarded their preference for (relatively expensive) cuts of meat which could be fried or grilled as wasteful and extravagant, and believed they should buy cheaper cuts and make them into stews and casseroles. American oven design, Atkinson argued, promoted energy-inefficient cooking practices. His Aladdin oven, which used a kerosene lamp and a fibreboard box, saved enormous amounts of fuel. Its drawbacks were that it took hours to heat up, lost much of its heat if the door was opened and took around five hours to cook most meat dishes. Moreover, the stews and casseroles to which it lent itself were less popular than fried and grilled meats in working-class households (Levenstein 1988:48).

Atkinson actively lobbied members of Congress to adopt the reform alliance's ideas, particularly Atwater's. He used the same

26

skills to promote his invention, giving public lectures at which Aladdin ovens were offered for sale. He also had an oven installed in the Massachusetts pavilion at the 1893 Columbia Exposition. The display featured a 'workingman's cottage' which incorporated all the reformers' ideas to demonstrate 'how a worker could live and eat well on $500 a year' (Levenstein 1988:52). In conjunction with the display, the Aladdin oven was used to serve cheap meals; printed menus displayed the nutritional values of the dishes served.

However, the Aladdin oven was anything but magical. By 1892 even some of the reform enthusiasts were telling Atkinson that it had technical problems: it was too expensive for the working class, and additional equipment was needed for frying and for boiling water. The very inefficiency of the traditional stove made it a valuable source of heating in winter. This was a task the Aladdin oven could not perform. In addition, just as with microwave ovens today, recipes had to be specially adapted for the Aladdin. An even more serious deficiency was the oven's potential to cause fires if left unattended (Levenstein 1988:54).

Atkinson's oven was out of touch with the lifestyle and needs of the people to whom it was marketed. Its inventor and promoters failed to understand the function of cooking equipment in working-class homes or to take into account popular methods of food preparation, assuming instead that cooking methods and menus would change to suit the equipment. Furthermore, Atkinson himself was known for his antagonistic relationship with organised labour.

THE NEW ENGLAND KITCHENS

The idea of serving meals prepared especially for workingmen, poor people and immigrants emerged from the collaboration of Ellen Richards, Atkinson, and Mary Abel, who was also interested in low-cost food for the poor. Abel had observed a public feeding program in Germany and written a prize-winning essay about her ideas on her return to the US, Richards, now the first woman faculty member at the Massachusetts Institute of Technology (MIT), was one of the judges for the essay competition, and Atkinson was a member of the MIT board. In 1889 the three saw an opportunity to promote both the Aladdin oven and food reform among the working class—and the New England Kitchen movement was born. The kitchens prepared take-away meals based on recipes developed and tested by Richards and her colleagues. From Boston, they spread to New York and other cities, where they were sometimes set up in conjunction with other reformist projects, particularly the settlement house movement, in which social workers lived in low-income communities and taught 'right living' ideas and skills.

Though the reformers were unable to assess the program's educational impact on poor people (i.e. its intended outcome), they noticed after six months that people were bringing cleaner containers to be filled (Levenstein 1988:50).

By 1891, Kitchen workers in Boston were already noticing a falling-off in patronage. However, they saw this not as indicative of deficiencies in the program but as testimony to the intractable problems of the people they were trying to help. There were nevertheless a couple of bright spots for the reformers. In 1892 the kitchen gained a contract to serve hot midday meals at all high schools in Boston and the first school lunch program began two years later. The reformers also believed that the kitchens had helped identify a group of people—upwardly mobile workers—who were receptive to their ideas. Their approach to dietary reform now shifted to a trickle-down theory. Since the original target group were not going to change, it was thought more sensible to work on improving the food choices of those who were inclined to adopt the 'New Nutrition'.

By 1900 the New England Kitchen movement was defunct, but the home economics movement was just starting to gain momentum. It would work to promote the establishment of school courses in domestic science incorporating much the same values as before but with the later addition of the management ideas associated with Frederick Taylor. Right living, Ellen Richards believed, was the fourth 'R' (Vincenti 1987).

The New England Kitchen movement illustrates a number of points which may be relevant to dietary change efforts today. Its organisers admitted that it failed to change the behaviour of poor and working-class people; certainly it did not have widespread or lasting influence. It never took hold outside the US and had disappeared entirely within a decade. Those kitchens, and the associated cooking schools and restaurants, that did persist for a time were changed by the people who patronised them. The clientele of the restaurants, for example, changed to city workers, who were more affluent.

THE ENGLISH FRYERS AND THE
STORY OF FISH AND CHIPS

A quite different example of communal food outlets for low-income and working-class people is the fish and chip shops of industrial England between 1870 and 1930.

These first emerged in working-class areas, where they produced inexpensive, mostly take-out meals for local residents. Their similarity to the New England Kitchens ends there, however. For one thing, they promoted a particular meal. In addition, they became enduringly popular both in their country of origin and as far afield as Australia and New Zealand. John Walton says the fish and chip trade in England influenced working-class diet, living standards and leisure and, at the beginning of the century, was clearly contributing to the British economy. It also, in his view, made a 'significant contribution to the political stability of inter-war Britain' (Walton 1989:243).

Referring to the trade journals of the 'fryers' during this period and an oral-history study of people in three Lancashire towns, Walton offers this summary of the most important effects of the trade on the working class:

> Fish and chips was an attractive meal which simply could not be made in most working-class kitchens; and it took cooking out of the home, which was a particular boon to the many families who lacked even the most basic items of kitchen technology. It reduced women's workloads and the general pressures of domestic labour, and thus may have reduced tensions in working-class families. The fish and chip shop became a centre for the exchange of gossip and sociability, and it opened its doors freely to women and children as well as men. So it came to fulfil a variety of important roles, as it helped to draw people into the wider life of the street and neighbourhood. (Walton 1989:259)

A fascinating range of people made the risky foray into the fish-frying business. Walton lists the previous occupations of 30 individuals who took up the trade. They included textile workers, engineers, an ex-navy NCO, and labourers (Walton 1989:250). He also notes that in some cases a woman engaged in frying to supplement her family's income and, when she did well at it, was joined on a full-time basis by her husband.

'Ownership' and interests served

It would be wrong to conclude, however, that the New England

Kitchens were simply failed welfare projects addressing social justice and health issues, while the fish and chip shops were jewels of private enterprise. Generally, those who controlled the Kitchens were not members of the community they served. They came from a different social group and believed that, in dietary knowledge and behaviour at least, they were superior to their 'consumers'. They thought they had what Peter Berger has graphically described as 'reality by the shortest possible hair' (Berger 1974:114). On the other hand, particularly in the late nineteenth century, many English people, often skilled tradesmen with relatively little capital, became fryers in their local neighbourhoods, sometimes starting out with frying as their second job.

Later it became more difficult to enter the trade because of high set-up costs associated with new technology, but by and large fish and chip shops were family businesses run by people who came from the same communities as their consumers or who at least were not divided from them by great social distance. In their own way, fryers may also have wished to change consumers' eating habits (to increase their sales) but the shops were building onto an already existing community practice, whereas the Kitchens were attempting to create a whole new pattern of meal selection and preparation.

Nor were the Kitchens purely social welfare efforts. They were associated with a commercial enterprise, the promotion of Aladdin ovens, and their funds came from private donors rather than government. It is not clear to what extent Aladdin oven promotion intruded on the Kitchens' work, but Levenstein notes that the Kitchen organisers blamed the project's demise, in part on Atkinson's failure to develop a container in which to carry hot food to homes.

Roles of men and women

Walton believes that women may have played a more important part in the frying trade than surviving records suggest. While it was expected that a fryer would be male and that, in a family business, his wife would assist him, some men came into the trade full time only after their wife had paved the way. The records of the fryers' trade organisation show that it was run by men, with women playing a traditional auxiliary role. In the case of the Kitchens, women played a more important role in management and decision making because of their association with the scientist-reformers who were to start the home economics movement. There were differences, too, in the gender balance of the two enterprises' customers. Some in the Kitchen movement saw their project as enticing poor and working-class men away from saloons and alcohol and their devastating effects on family budgets. There is a hint in Levenstein's work that men were not overly keen on the type of food the Kitchens served. Walton suggests that, although fish and chips was a family meal, men were given larger serves, or perhaps the fish, whereas children tended to have chips without fish. In addition, the shops' busiest periods were around 11 p.m., when men's clubs closed, and at lunchtime on Saturday, when many men went to the football (Walton 1989:255). On the other hand, particularly in textile towns in the north of England, where both parents often worked, bought meals freed women for domestic chores other than cooking.

Changes over time

The Kitchens' clientele gradually changed from the original target group, the poor and the working class, to the middle class and city office and shop workers. The take-out portion of the operation settled into a pattern of supplying hospitals and schools. The restaurants and coffee shops attached to some Kitchens gradually attracted students and businessmen.

As public health regulations stiffened, technology improved and customers became choosier, fish and chip shop proprietors faced increasing set-up and operating costs, and it became much less likely that a poor family would improve its lot or its social status through the frying trade. The trade also became increasingly professionalised, which made it even less likely to be a route out of waged work. But the fish and chip shops never lost their original clientele, even as they won customers among the middle and upper class.

Views of health experts

Whereas the New England Kitchens were set up to achieve goals set for them by nutrition experts, fish and chip shops from the very beginning had antagonistic relations with authorities. Upper-class people complained about the smells of fish and cooking fat. Public health officials were concerned about the hygiene of the shops, and about the failure of their working-class women customers to prepare healthy foods for their families. Walton sees these attacks as stemming from prejudices (about working-class lifestyles) disguised as science.

Relationship to communities

Fish and chip shops seem to have been a social focus as well as fast food outlets and they were so dispersed as to be a feature of quite small sub-neighbourhoods. In some areas, at the peak of their popularity, there was estimated to be 'one [shop] to every two or three substantial working-class streets' (Walton 1989:247). Kitchens, on the other hand, were planned so they would not become a focus for social life. Their promoters believed the family home was the place where Americans would want to eat, and this was the rationale for making the Kitchens a take-out service (Levenstein 1988:52).

Ethnicity

The Kitchen organisers found ethnic communities especially tough to deal with. They sought out, for example, predominantly Jewish and black localities in which to establish Kitchens, as it was generally believed at that time that these groups had particular difficulty adopting healthy eating habits. There is little in either Preistland's or Walton's accounts of the fish and chip trade to throw light on this issue, but Walton does mention the tradition of Italian families in Glasgow running fish and chip restaurants. One thing both the Kitchens and the shops seem to have had in common was the risk of fire. In the shops it was a hazard of working with hot fat, and Levenstein notes that an Aladdin oven left unattended could burn through the table it was resting on.

In the examples of the Kitchens and the English fish and chip shops, we have on the one hand a program based on a questionable rationale which contributed nutritionally to the poor for a limited period and in a few locations, and on the other hand a cottage industry with no nutritional pretensions which probably made a significant nutritional, social and economic contribution. Both examples had problems as well as possibilities, but conventional, expert-driven Good Nutrition is obviously only one way to improve lives and health in the community.

WHAT ARE THE LIMITATIONS OF EXPERT-DRIVEN GOOD NUTRITION PROGRAMS?

Many valuable aspects of working-class community life may go unrecognised by middle-class professionals. Worse still, they may be rejected on the basis of a value judgment disguised as a scientific assessment. It is important to recognise vested interests if one is to understand why things happen the way they do and why some groups hold particular points of view.

The sociologist Peter Berger, who has written on ethical aspects of social policy in relation to Third World development, argues lucidly that there are great problems attached to dogmatism (of both the right and the left) in development policy. Berger sees the role of the sociologist as being to clarify the vested interests of actors by placing their ideas in a social context (Berger 1989:1). He counsels a cautious approach to political action and believes that sociology can be used to help make morally responsible decisions by revealing the vested interests which often lie behind the rhetoric. Taking such an approach to analysing specific dietary guidance does not, of course, tell us what is scientifically 'correct'. All it can do is make clear the connection between particular ideas and interests.

The discussion of historical aspects of scientific dietary guidance and the description of some programs which flowed from the New Nutrition in the US demonstrate that, regardless of their technical merits and health consequences, nutrition programs like all political actions, represent a range of vested interests. As Berger points out, to recognise this is liberating rather than crippling, as it helps us make what he calls moral judgments about programs. He refers to this as striking a morally defensible balance between having power and doing good. Berger speaks of a 'calculus of pain' (Berger 1974:137). He advocates calculating the cost of a policy by assuming that it is inevitable that someone will pay a price and asking whether the causation of that pain is morally defensible.

Are Good Nutrition programs valuable? Do they have problems which outweigh the benefits? To answer these questions, typical Good Nutrition programs must be interrogated beyond their technical and scientific aspects. We need, then, to ask of any such programs not only, Did people eat (for example) less fat as a result? but also, and with equal assiduousness, Was anyone hurt by the program? and, Is this particular effect of the program ethically defensible? Berger differentiates between an ethic of attitude and an ethic of responsibility. An ethic of attitude makes concessions for the pain that follows a particular social action in the belief that what really matters morally is the attitude of the actor. In this view, problems created by a policy are defensible as long as the policy's intention was morally sound. However, Berger believes that an ethic of responsibility is the only ethic with which those who seek to be politically effective can operate. A good moral intention in creating nutrition policy is not enough. Responsibility must be taken for the policy's consequences regardless of intentions.

> . . . an ethic of responsibility must be cautious, calculating a perennially uncertain mass of means, costs and consequences. This is tedious and endlessly frustrating, which is why so many people, especially young people, are drawn to an ethic of attitude: moral purity is one of the cheapest human achievements. (Berger 1989:7)

4

Good Nutrition as a mixture of culture and science

 Good Nutrition consists of a core of science in a cultural 'package'. Just as Atwater's food composition studies, for example, were wrapped in his socio-religious views, Good Nutrition is a form of wisdom which draws on science but which is ultimately one view about what is best. Wisdom is the product of human experience and tradition rather than being scientifically discovered 'truth'. This is a good reason for opening up Good Nutrition to wider debate and participation and not leaving it as the exclusive province of medical and nutrition experts.

The cultural packaging of Good Nutrition is well illustrated by the nutrition advice given during the Second World War, particularly in the United States, but also in Australia and the United Kingdom, when people were expected to eat what would benefit the Allied cause. Although patriotic sentiment is no longer invoked, the basic foods recommended remain essentially the same as they were 50 years ago. Since the food humans eat must always satisfy the same biological needs, this cannot be otherwise. Yet while our constitutional needs for nutrients do not change, the 'packaging' of Good Nutrition does.

In thinking about Good Nutrition as 'messages', it is useful to differentiate between the content and the context. The content, the actual foods recommended, cannot vary very much. The foods must be of the types needed for survival, and they must be both available and acceptable. The seven-food-group guidelines of the 1940s in the US are almost identical with the dietary guidelines endorsed for Australians in the 1990s.

Three eggs a week, for example, seems to have enduring allure as a dietary recommendation, having survived from the food grouping era into the later coronary disease prevention phase. In the 1940s people were told to 'Eat at least three eggs per week'; in the 1980s it was 'Eat no more than three eggs per week'. At least three eggs a week because they are 'good'; no more than three eggs a week because they are 'bad'. The same basic recommendation is wrapped in two different Good Nutrition packages.

If Good Nutrition is indeed culturally packaged, what influences create the packaging and how does it change over time? In particular, how did coronary heart disease prevention become the packaging of the 1980s?

There is already a view in the community that many healthy eating messages are transitory. One often hears complaints that what was once a 'no-no' food for dieters is now highly recommended. Bread and potatoes, for example, formerly listed among the foods to be eaten in small amounts if at all, are now lauded for the contribution they can make to a slimming diet. Those who complain about these shifts in Good Nutrition messages usually target experts, wishing they would 'make up their minds' or that they would agree among themselves about the 'truth' of the matter. However, finding some kind of gold standard of truth in nutrition may be impossible. Scientists cannot establish a Good Nutrition 'fact' by a laboratory experiment or a medical study. Good Nutrition represents a contemporary point of view, not an immutable truth.

Facts are transformed and passed through a number of filters before they become Good Nutrition advice. Identifying just whose view a piece of advice is based on, how it was developed, and how that particular view came to prominence is the key to understanding contemporary Good Nutrition.

In the marketplace, food manufacturers or food producers promote their products by selectively using those Good Nutrition messages that serve their commercial interests. Breakfast cereal manufacturers are not likely to broadcast messages about the value of breastfeeding, for example. Social responsibility is secondary to commercial intent. The Good Nutrition messages which are most likely to be filtered out are those which may inhibit sales of a particular product or product line. Fibre from fruit and vegetables, for example, is presently thought to be more beneficial than cereal fibre. This information is understandably not likely to be put on breakfast cereal packets.

The 1992 revision of the Dietary Guidelines for Australians

36

Recommended foods have barely changed over 50 years

NUTRITION EXPERTS URGE
US TO EAT THESE FOODS
EVERY DAY

Note that "salad makings" occur in several of the categories

MILK—at least a pint for everyone, more for children—or cheese, or evaporated or dried milk.

ORANGES, TOMATOES, GRAPEFRUIT, OR RAW CABBAGE—at least one of these.

VEGETABLES—GREEN, LEAFY, AND YELLOW—one big helping or more—some raw, some cooked.

POTATOES AND APPLES—and other vegetables and fruits.

LEAN MEAT, POULTRY, OR FISH—or sometimes dried beans or peas.

EGGS—at least 3 or 4 a week, cooked any way you choose or in "made" dishes.

BREAD AND CEREAL—whole grain products or enriched bread and flour.

FATS, SWEETS, and seasonings as you like them.

US recommended foods, 1943

included extra advice on the intake of two nutrients, iron and calcium. This advice was directed particularly at women but also at athletes and other groups. The recommendation on iron was taken up by the Australian Meat and Livestock Corporation (AMLC), the marketing and research arm of the red meat industry in Australia. A report on the AMLC's nutrition-based promotional campaign illustrates some of the problems of Good Nutrition programs directed by vested interests (Tolisson 1992). It notes that the campaign was directed at women because their meat consumption had been declining. The AMLC claimed that 70 per cent of women did not consume the recommended intake of iron and as a result felt tired. A black-and-white television advertisement featured a series of tired-looking women expressing doubt about the adequacy of their iron consumption. (According to Tolisson, as a consequence of the campaign, the proportion of women who were fairly confident about their iron intake fell from 62 per cent to 54 per cent.)

This is at least a bit less crude than the TV advertisement of the equivalent New Zealand campaign, in which a depressed, presumably iron-deficient woman standing on the edge of a cliff is brought back from the brink by eating meat!

Women feel tired for many reasons other than low meat con-

Australian Good Nutrition: 1950s compared with the 1990s

Group	Basic Five Food Groups c1950 (A foundation diet) Serves/day	CSIRO Healthy Diet Pyramid 1991 (A total diet) Serves/day
Bread/cereal	4	6–8
Vegetable/fruit	4	7
Meat	1	1
Milk	300 ml (adults) 600 ml (children)	600 ml
Butter/table margarine	1 tablespoon	included in 'extras'
	Enjoy a variety of foods from each of these five food groups every day in the amounts shown. Extra servings depend on your size, activity and age.	Variety still encouraged. A total rather than a minimum diet.

sumption, as a TV comedy sketch which lampooned the AMLC advertisement caustically pointed out. Though in the commercial world Good Nutrition is readily seen as part of marketing, this is not generally thought to apply to campaigns organised by health authorities, governments, heart disease and cancer societies, community health centres and universities. However, among these organisations, too, the motives for becoming involved in campaigns of persuasion can vary from the idealistic, such as helping people be healthier, to the pragmatic, such as making an organisation better known in the community. Probably most Good Nutrition campaigns are driven by a mixture of motives. In one recent instance, an American health education consultant to Australian hospitals proposed that a measure of the success of health education for hospital outpatients with heart problems should be the proportion who returned to the hospital for triple-bypass surgery. The reasoning may have been that providing 'education' for patients favourably impresses them.

While the consultant did not propose that health education programs be run solely to attract business to hospitals, medical and health organisations, as well as the commercial sector, can and do use Good Nutrition as a marketing or public relations strategy.

If Good Nutrition can be used for a number of purposes,

Wartime arouses particular nutrition anxieties

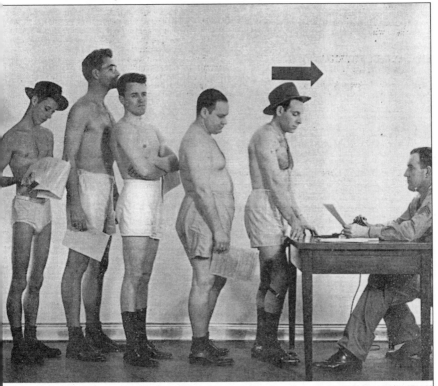

BUY WAR BONDS AND STAMPS

What's wrong with America's health?

Doctors, editors, congressmen and many a thoughtful citizen are deeply concerned by the same stark fact: *40% of America's young men are unfit for military service.*★

This doesn't make us a nation of weaklings. Ask our enemies! And it's no reflection on the men themselves. Most of them are serving in other ways. *But it does show America's health is far below what it should be.*

Three chief remedies have been suggested—preventive medicine, physical training, and diet. The last is often overlooked. But it has been officially estimated that *about ⅓ of all Selective Service rejections are caused directly or indirectly by nutritional deficiencies* — lack of food or improper food.

That's one big reason for the government's food education program. It's one reason why schools and factories regularly serve milk to their students and workers. For milk is nature's most nearly perfect food. Surgeon-General Parran recommends "a pint a day for adults, a quart for children."

At National Dairy, we are doing our best to protect and improve the quality of milk and its many products—while our laboratories develop milk in other new forms that will benefit everybody.

Dedicated to the wider use and better understanding of dairy products as human food . . . as a base for the development of new products and materials . . . as a source of health and enduring progress on the farms and in the towns and cities of America.

NATIONAL DAIRY
PRODUCTS CORPORATION
AND AFFILIATED COMPANIES

★ *Report of Senate Subcommittee on Wartime Health and Education, January 2, 1945.*

including to achieve organisational goals, it should not be too surprising that the wider culture can also influence the content and style of Good Nutrition messages. An organisation might promote a given nutritional message for a number of reasons, but could social or political influences select the message itself? Why is 'Eat less fat' perhaps the most frequently heard Good Nutrition message?

THE PACKAGING OF GOOD NUTRITION

In wartime, when whole countries are organised around defending their national interests and perhaps their very existence, the effort intrudes into almost every corner of society, including Good Nutrition. The impact of the Second World War on Good Nutrition in the United States is well documented in contemporary issues of the *Journal of the American Dietetic Association*. As in the First World War, the health of conscripts was a major source of public concern prompted by the number of young men rejected by the military on medical grounds. Poor diet was seen as part of the reason for this problem. In addition, Good Nutrition for civilians was seen as essential to ensure a healthy workforce for wartime production, both agricultural and military-industrial.

In 1942 the *Journal* published a description of the US government's intended National Industrial Nutrition Program. An article in the same journal 32 years later described the program thus:

> The theme of the 1942 national industrial program became the title of the food guide: 'U.S. Needs Us Strong—Eat Nutritional Food'. The overall objective of the program was to obtain 'full health returns from the nation's food resources . . . for victory . . . and when the war is won' in order to promote optimum nutrition through wise food selection for war workers and the population at home. (Hertzler & Anderson 1974)

The goal of the program was to conserve human resources as well as increase production and it had three 'fronts', industry, homes and communities. It was linked with the Office of Defense Health and Welfare Services, the War Manpower Commission and the US Public Health Service. The Public Health Service had set up a nutrition advisory service which included one woman, Ernestine Perry, who had organised one of the first industrial nutrition campaigns at the community level. An anonymous writer in the *Journal* that same year observed:

> The belief, too widespread, that a biochemist, a surgeon, or an

Food producing can be a patriotic activity

Sow the seeds of Victory!
plant & raise your own vegetables

WRITE TO THE NATIONAL WAR GARDEN COMMISSION ~ WASHINGTON, D.C. for free books on gardening, canning & drying

"Every Garden a Munition Plant"
Charles Lathrop Pack, President .

internist, even though well versed in the sciences ancillary to the art of dietetics and distinguished in his field but knowing little or nothing of actual cookery, is capable of supervising the infinite technical details involved in managing a kitchen and kitchen help, is probably as fallacious as the idea that a metallurgist, because of his knowledge of the various metals of which a plane is constructed, could competently supervise the operation and maintenance of a flying fortress. (JADA 1942:756)

In launching the campaign, Paul McNutt, administrator of the Office of Defense Health and Welfare Services and chairman of the

Victory meals: patriotic *and* nutritious

A VICTORY LUNCH

Those attending the recent annual meeting of the National Council of Women in New York were served a "Victory Lunch," the menu for which was prepared by Mrs. Elizabeth Bussing and endorsed by the Nutrition Committee of Greater New York. The meal, described as a "war meal," was prepared with four requirements in mind: to use foods which are plentiful and which are not needed by the Army and the Navy; to feed the family correctly; to ease the load on the family budget; and to prove that a cheap nutritious meal, made up of less familiar foods, can be attractive and appetizing. (The cost of the meal per person as purchased in retail markets in New York on November 18 was 13 cents.)

The items which made up the menu were: Kale Soup, Chili Soy Beans, Cabbage Salad with Wheat Sprouts, Whole Wheat Rolls, Whole Wheat Apple Scallop, and coffee or milk.

The notes regarding the menu, which, together with a food chart were distributed to those present, contained the following information assembled by Dr. Clara Taylor of Teachers College, Columbia University:

Why kale? Freight-car space is needed for troop supplies. Many of the fresh green vegetables to which we are accustomed simply won't be available in usual quantities. Kale is grown in most parts of the country; doesn't need to be shipped. Kale is one of the most inexpensive vegetables, about 8 cents a pound in New York now.

Why soy beans? Meat must be saved for the fighting forces. Soy beans are a meat substitute. Moreover, soy beans give nitrogen to the soil in which they grow. This saves commercial nitrogen for explosives needed by our armed forces. Soy beans have a high protein content. Soy beans can be bought for 8 to 10 cents a pound on the New York market.

Why apples? Apples today are a Victory Special and are produced locally all over the United States. Like all fruits, they give us some of the protective factors. They are economical.

Why wheat sprouts? See above under kale. Grain sprouts are a rich source of vitamin C. Wheat for home sprouting is available at local feed stores for a few cents a pound.

To sprout wheat, it was explained, secure high-grade wheat seed from seedsmen and local grain dealers. The sprouts may be obtained by germinating the wheat on a wire shelf covered with a moist cloth and placed over water in a wide, shallow, covered vessel. At room temperature the sprouts are about one inch long and ready to eat in one week.

By means of a chart it was demonstrated that the luncheon contributed about three-eighths of the calories needed for one day. More than three-fourths of the protein, five-eighths of the calcium, almost the full amounts of iron and vitamin B, and the full amounts of vitamin A, C, and G, plus a generous and desirable surplus of vitamins A and C.

It was suggested that the delegates to the meeting give similar luncheons or dinners in their own localities and that help in planning menus adapted to local food supplies could be obtained from local nutrition committees, the Red

Cross, the Department of Agriculture, or the home economics departments of colleges. The ingredients of two dishes served at the Victory Lunch and directions for preparing are given below:

Danish Kale Soup

Potatoes, medium-sized, 4	Salt, ½ tsp.
Milk, 1 qt.	Pepper, dash
Onions, medium-sized, sliced, 2	Kale, ¼ lb.
Butter *or* fortified margarine, 2 tbsp.	

Peel potatoes, cook in boiling salted water until tender and put through ricer. Meantime scald milk and onions together in double-boiler for 15 minutes. Strain out onions, add hot potatoes and seasoning. Wash kale and remove stems; put through food chopper using fine knife. Add to soup just before serving. Serve topped with sour cream if desired. Makes 6 servings.

Chili Soy Beans

Soy beans, 1 lb.	Meat drippings, 2 tbsp.
Beef, ground, ½ lb.	Salt, 1 tsp.
Onion, diced, 1½ cups	Tomatoes, cooked, 3½ cups
Garlic, minced, 2 cloves	(No. 2½ can)
Green pepper, diced, 1	Chili powder, 1½ to 2 tsp.

Wash soy beans and cover with water and let soak overnight. Add 1 teaspoon salt and additional water to cover and simmer covered 3 hours or until tender. Sauté beef, onion, garlic and green pepper in meat drippings until lightly browned. Add salt and tomatoes, simmer about 30 minutes or until thick. Add chili powder and drained soy beans. Heat well, serve in individual casseroles.

War Manpower Commission, nominated the home 'front' where eight million workers' lunches were made, as a 'vital point of attack'. He made it clear that it was considered an important wartime task for women to provide 'strength and health protection' for men by making these lunches from 'right food' (*JADA* 1942:596).

Education materials prepared by wartime nutritionists and dietitians bore titles such as 'Fightin' food', 'Make America strong' and 'Fight food waste in the home' (*JADA* 1942:756–757).

Wartime Good Nutrition encouraged people to become food producers as well as consumers, of vegetables in particular. The tradition of 'Victory Gardens' begun in the First World War was restarted in both the US and Britain to this end and a program of Victory meals was established in the US. People were encouraged not to waste food, to conserve excess produce and to put up with shortages of foods that were being diverted to feed troops and to supply Allied countries suffering food shortages. Levenstein notes that 40 per cent of the US's vegetables in 1943 were produced in local gardens in backyards and community plots (Levenstein 1993:85). Britain too mounted a successful campaign with the slogan 'Dig for Victory'. This worked towards achieving self sufficiency in produce which had formerly been imported but supplies of which had been drastically cut by German U-boat attacks on merchant shipping (Davies 1993).

The cultural portion of Good Nutrition in the 1940s in both the US and Britain was about supporting the war effort. The basic foods recommended did not differ very much from those recommended today, but the levers used to encourage people to follow the guide were largely patriotic ones. Women today are encouraged to prepare meals that will help fight heart disease; in the 1940s the rationale for selecting basically the same foods was that they would help obtain victory over the enemy of that era.

> Never waste anything, however small. Never eat more than enough. You'll be fitter, you'll save money, you'll make cargo space available for materials of war. Every time you cook you can help or hinder Hitler! (UK Ministry of Food pamphlet in Davies 1993)

Meat supplies were limited during the war and governments encouraged people to reduce their meat consumption by both educational and policy strategies. Margaret Mead, the famous anthropologist, played an important wartime role as executive secretary of the US National Research Council's Committee on Food Habits, which advised the government. In an article in the *Journal of the American Dietetic Association*, Mead speculates about the best way to embed a message ('Eat less meat') in a social context to achieve a desirable outcome in people's behaviour and beliefs.

She considers the possibility of either telling people that too much meat is bad for them and that therefore they should eat less, or, alternatively, of portraying science as providing substitute dietary components that would allow people to deal with the meat shortage. She notes the strong correlation of social status with meat consumption and discusses how this should be addressed (*JADA* 1943:189). This is an example of the conscious 'tailoring' of the cultural packaging of a particular behaviour which the government of the day wanted to promote.

The policy issue of meat consumption connected the UK, the US and Australia during the war. The then Australian director of army catering, Brigadier Sir Cedric Stanton Hicks, recounts how the British prime minister, Winston Churchill, saw the availability of meat as important to civilian and military morale and the war effort

(Stanton Hicks 1972). Meat rations were small (two ounces per person per day in 1944), and Churchill considered that if they could be increased, the populace would be convinced that the German U-boat threat to food supplies was being contained. A barrier in the way of this strategy was the amount of Australian-produced meat that the American armed forces were consuming. Churchill wanted a larger share of Australian meat for Britain. Stanton Hicks describes the mixture of nutritional, technical and military arguments that he used in a diplomatically difficult mission to persuade the US military to reduce food waste. Like Mead, he juggled the semantics. He thought 'food conservation' inappropriate as it was 'an intolerable notion in our Citizen Armies' and chose instead to promote to the US military hierarchy the concept of proper 'food utilisation' as part of an officer's duty to ensure the men under his command were well fed.

CONTROL AND CONSERVATION: ENDURING THEMES IN GOOD NUTRITION

The themes of control and conservation recur in Good Nutrition and probably represent basic survival anxieties. Whereas in the 1940s self-control and conservation of resources were advocated for patriotic reasons, today conservation and self-control may be understood in ecological terms. In a recent report on Jennifer Davies' book *The Wartime Kitchen and Garden*, Anne Boston comments that what was learned from wartime experiences of 'salvage and self-sufficiency' may be useful in terms of today's problems of pollution and waste (Boston 1993:103).

Some nutritionists are already advocating the ecological approach to Good Nutrition. Two American nutritionists have developed 'Guidelines for sustainability' (Gussow & Clancy 1986) and the Australian government's Food and Nutrition Policy of 1992 includes, under the broader concept of chronic disease prevention, a section on 'sustainable development'.

Many models are conceivable, given the fundamental nature of food and the range of concerns that exist in industrialised societies. A form of Good Nutrition based on social justice values, for example, could easily accommodate the themes of self-control and conservation of resources but give different reasons for their importance. These might be based on the idea of redistributing resources to those who have little, and might include campaigns to reduce the cost of fruit and vegetables so poorer people could afford to eat more of them. The Good Nutrition messages might emphasise 'simple foods' and moralise about conspicuous consumption and the profligacy of the rich instead of focusing on poor people's inability to manage their resources.

If the packaging (as distinct from the biological-needs core) of Good Nutrition is dynamic rather than static, composed of a set of themes, some of which (control and conservation), may be common to all Western societies, why do some themes become more important than others? Are there conditions which predispose to change? How was the packaging of Good Nutrition transformed from patriotism to heart disease prevention?

A TRANSITION IN DIETARY GUIDANCE

During the 1970s, the then-dominant model—the 'food group' approach—was criticised for its inadequacies and replaced by a different model—the 'dietary guidelines' approach. The food group idea was developed in the early part of this century and arrived in Australia (in terms of being officially embraced by the health authorities) in the 1950s. Clements notes that before the 1950s, advice was general rather than specific, emphasising liberal intake of foods considered 'protective', such as milk, eggs, fruit and vegetables. Importantly, according to Clements, this advice also urged moderation in the consumption of carbohydrates and fats (Clements 1986:218).

Although Clements pinpoints the 'first important development', that is the development in the US of the 'four basic food groups' in the late 1950s, the first American national food guide based on a food group system dates from 1916. It is especially noteworthy that two versions of the same information appeared. One, couched in household terms, was developed by a woman, Caroline Hunt, for other women; the other, based on nutrients, was presented to the scientific community by her boss, C.F. Langworthy. Hunt classified food into five groups:

milk, meat, fish, poultry, eggs, and meat substitutes,
bread and other cereal foods,
butter and wholesome fats,
vegetables and fruits, and
simple sweets.
(Hertzler & Anderson 1974)

The Australian version of the food group concept also had five groups. The distinguishing characteristics of such embodiments of Good Nutrition are that they refer to foods rather than nutrients, that they try to ensure that people obtain minimum nutritional requirements, and that their basic concern is to prevent nutritionally deficient diets. They focus on preventing insufficiency of food intake or excessively narrow choices, the latter probably the origin of the term a 'balanced' diet.

Hertzler and Anderson's discussion of these systems' development over the next two decades clearly demonstrates the domestic themes underlying them (Hertzler & Anderson 1974). They were family focused: sometimes expressed in terms of amounts of foods needed by an 'average' family for one week, directed at the 'homemaker', and concerned that the energy needs of the family were met. Just as clearly, new laboratory-acquired scientific knowledge about vitamins and minerals influenced the underlying themes of Good Nutrition.

In 1941 the first recommended dietary allowances (RDAs) for Americans (perhaps more correctly nutrient allowances, because they do not refer to foods) were the scientific justification for increasing the number of food groups to eight (subsequently seven). At this time, although the biological basis of nutrition was becoming clearer, the wartime appeal to patriotism dominated the public face of Good Nutrition. By 1956 the US Department of Agriculture had opted for just four groups.

If models of Good Nutrition are like paradigms of science, some of the explanations of change put forward by the historian and philosopher of science Thomas Kuhn should be useful. For example, a current explanation or model may not be satisfactory in some way. The scientists working within the model find it unable to either explain or provide an understanding of a particular problem. Once confidence is lost in the current model a new one may take over. In science, as Chalmers notes, competing paradigms identify different questions as important and have different standards which clash (Chalmers 1982:95).

Chalmers goes on to say that in Kuhnian terms there is no particular reason why a rational scientist should choose one or another of competing paradigms. Different scientists base their choice on the differing priority they give to various factors, and they use different standards to judge a model, depending on their interests or what they consider important. Chalmers concludes that although there are various reasons why one model of science comes

47

to be competition with others, there is no 'logically compelling argument' why a scientist might choose one model in preference to another (Chalmers 1982:97). The revolution is complete when enough scientists in the area in question abandon the old ideas to take up the new. Adherents to the previous model are now marginalised, out of the mainstream.

This way of thinking can be applied to changing models of Good Nutrition and contributes to an understanding of the shift from food groups to dietary guidelines as the public face of Good Nutrition.

Food grouping systems were available in the US from early in the century until the 1970s, and in Australia from the mid-1950s until the late 1970s. From 1941 onwards in the US and from the mid-1950s in Australia, the food group concept was extended, using the latest biological information, through recommended dietary allowances, which set out the amount of various vitamins, minerals and other nutrients needed for a nutritionally adequate diet. There are relatively minor variations in these allowances between the two countries. Criticism of the US food grouping system began in the late 1960s and continued into the 1970s, when food groups were largely supplanted by the dietary guidelines approach.

5

Dietary guidelines

Inconsistencies between available information and its use in social action indicate that in some programs, cultural issues are powerful enough to overcome empirical data. The packaging becomes the message. For example, few studies on diet and heart disease include women, but this is not acknowledged when changed behaviour is pressed on the whole community. The dietary prevention of coronary disease illustrates the dissonance between formal knowledge and its applications, when cultural imperatives overpower more circumspect approaches.

The genesis of the US dietary guidelines is central to an understanding of the politics of nutrition and the roles of powerful interests in producing national nutritional goals. The influential 1974 recommendations of the Senate Select Committee on Nutrition and Human Needs chaired by Senator George McGovern differed from the guidelines the Scandinavian countries developed in the late 1960s. It would have been quite possible for the Australian guidelines to have been different again in both their detail and their rationale. However, Australia adopted the American approach and preventing the 'epidemic of killer diseases' became the dominant rationale for Good Nutrition in Australia too.

The chief concern in developing the early food grouping systems was that people 'balance' their food consumption so as to obtain enough energy from protein, fat and carbohydrate while also consuming adequate amounts of vitamins and minerals. It is possible to infer here an effort to correct the error of the Atwater years, when the focus was on getting enough protein and energy at a time before the existence of vitamins was discovered. In that version of Good Nutrition, such foods as fruits and vegetables were not promoted—indeed they were frowned upon as unnecessary luxuries for those who had little money.

Food grouping systems after the Second World War taught a basic minimum diet and assumed that people would eat more than this to meet their energy needs, particularly if they were physically active.

In the late 1960s and early 1970s, debate arose which sought to re-emphasise concerns about overconsumption of energy, especially from fat. Whereas previously undernutrition had been the focus, now a series of studies which focused on possible links between heart disease and fat consumption, particularly in affluent countries, led to the McGovern Committee's 1977 publication of 'Dietary Goals for the United States'. Although this was not a government document, many accepted it as having the US government's imprimatur. It was not until 1980 that the official 'Dietary Guidelines for Americans' was produced jointly by the departments of Agriculture and Health and Human Services.

Scandinavian countries had produced similar advice for their citizens in the late 1960s, but this did not receive comparable coverage in international medical and nutrition journals. Wide reporting of the American developments and the ensuing, often acrimonious, debate ensured that the original, unofficial 'Dietary Goals' would remain the reference point for many countries as they developed their own goals and guidelines.

This would seem to be a reasonable basis for assuming that what happened in the US had more influence on Australia than the earlier European developments. This is also probably true for the UK.

Professor Stewart Truswell has defined dietary guidelines as:

> . . . recommendations by an expert committee or group which suggests ways in which the present average diet of an affluent country could be improved as a contribution to reducing or delaying coronary and other cardiovascular and degenerative diseases. (Truswell 1983:7)

Dietary guidelines differ in important ways from advice based on food groups. First, guidelines address the present average diet of the citizens of an affluent country, and their 'success' should logically be measured in those terms. Second, they are expected 'to make a contribution' to reducing the prevalence or delaying certain kinds of disease, with the emphasis on heart disease. They are not expected by themselves, however, to eliminate heart disease nor to alter its incidence.

Food groups, on the other hand, address individuals' food selection. They are about the food choices of one day, and are not associated with the prevention of any particular disease. They fit more comfortably into the category 'health promotion', while dietary guidelines fall into the category of 'disease prevention'.

The change from a form of Good Nutrition based on food groups to one based on dietary guidelines is therefore an important transition with practical implications. The rationale for the dietary guidelines approach rests on epidemiological research, that is research on whole populations. Without arguing here about the strengths or weaknesses of this approach, the dietary guidelines rationale has been developed from an argument that those countries which have a high national average consumption of fat have high rates of heart disease. The reasoning goes that if the national average fat consumption can be reduced, heart disease statistics should improve.

Clinical studies on smaller groups of specially selected subjects have looked at this same issue, asking: Do groups with high average fat consumption have higher rates of heart disease (usually heart attacks and related problems)? And, if the fat content in the diet of a group is reduced, will members of that group have fewer heart attacks than people whose dietary fat has not been reduced? In this model the mediating factor of interest between dietary fat and heart attacks is the blood cholesterol level. Much research is also devoted to this mediating relationship. This research asks: Do people who eat more fat have higher blood cholesterol levels?

Complicated questions are involved in the relationship of dietary fat to blood cholesterol, the relationship of blood cholesterol to heart disease, and the relationship of dietary fat to heart disease. When intervention programs are mounted to reduce heart disease, further questions arise: Will lower-fat diets lead to lower blood cholesterol levels?, Will lowering blood cholesterol reduce heart attacks? and thus Will lower-fat diets reduce heart attacks? If the answer to these questions is yes, a further layer of complexity is added in considering whether particular public intervention programs are effective in achieving changed diets, either by persuading people to alter their food choices or by modifying the food supply.

For the dietary guidelines to lead to success in public health terms affirmative answers are needed to the following questions:

51

1. Will a lower fat content in the national average diet lead to a lower national average blood cholesterol level?
2. Will a lower national average blood cholesterol level lead to fewer heart attacks?
3. Are intervention programs resulting in changed diets and changed health outcomes?

At the population level, all three questions remain unanswered. They will never be unequivocally answered, because it is too difficult and too expensive to do the necessary research. Many scientists currently working in this area would say that, based on research in much smaller groups, the answer to these questions is yes, although some would disagree. Moreover, the effectiveness of dietary change in preventing heart disease is not the only diet–health issue, nor indeed is it necessarily the most important diet–health issue. These are questions of policy, not of science.

Internationally, famine and child malnutrition are still present in catastrophic proportions. In Australia, as elsewhere, women still have the responsibility for feeding babies and children and worry about this. Many older people have difficulty getting to shops and preparing meals for themselves. The concern with being overweight is not only a medical one but, in societies like our own, hooks in millions of women to expensive commercial programs and unhealthy eating practices. How did heart disease and dietary guidelines rise to the top of the nutrition problems table and come to dominate Good Nutrition on an international scale? Perhaps because they are underpinned by a fear of death, which takes priority over quality of life concerns? Perhaps because heart disease is above all an issue for middle-aged men, the group which dominates most social institutions and policy-making? Or perhaps because diet-related diseases have been said to cost the nation one-third of its health expenditure (Better Health Commission Taskforce on Nutrition 1987).

A TRANSITION OF CONCERNS: THE CHRONIC DISEASE ERA

Concern about heart disease and its possible association with diet rose after the Second World War. Ancel Keys was responsible for the first study which made international comparisons of fat consumption and heart disease rates. He came to the conclusion that higher rates occurred in countries with the highest fat consumption and highest standards of living. Interestingly, Keys' recent explanation of the shift in focus from underconsumption to overconsumption and heart disease gives the media a role in publicising class and gender-based beliefs: 'As the war ended the public media reported other than war casualties; prominent men were dying from heart attacks' (Keys 1990:288). The first dietary study of middle-aged male executives was under way as early as 1948.

Mark Hegsted, a prominent figure in nutrition research (and a central figure in the release of the first 'Dietary Goals for the United States' in 1974), sees a couple of steps in this shift in focus. In some recent reflections on the history of nutrition, he observes that scientists tend to work on a particular topic until it becomes 'exhausted', and then shift their research focus elsewhere. First, he says, a focus on obesity and protein/calorie malnutrition 'rescued' nutrition from the 'exhaustion of the vitamin era'. Obesity and malnutrition presumably gave researchers a fresh goal after the vitamins had been sorted out. Neither obesity nor protein/calorie malnutrition, he notes, 'had a very illustrious history' (Hegsted, 1990:284). Presumably this means that they never became really exciting areas of research where great advances were made and difficult problems solved. Certainly neither obesity nor malnutrition has abated as a result of this research.

Death rates from heart disease fell during the war and rose after it, leading scientists to speculate that this might be related to food scarcity during the war and abundance after it. In Hegsted's terms, the 'new era' of nutrition was beginning.

During the 1960s, the McGovern Committee conducted hearings on poverty and malnutrition in the US. Hegsted identifies the latter as one of the areas in nutrition research which by that time had become 'exhausted'. Almost as if looking for another area to develop, the committee then developed an interest in chronic disease. Some hearings it held on what were referred to as the 'killer diseases' led to the development of the 'Dietary Goals for the United States'. The McGovern Committee's release of the second version of its 'Dietary Goals' in 1977 was reported in medical and nutrition journals. Some commentators were critical of the report's specific recommendations, its omissions (including that of overweight as a concern), and its scientific basis.

Michele Zebiche, a political scientist who studied this transition period, also attributed the change of focus from under- to overnutrition to the committee's report. She concluded that the main influences on the committee members were political ones: the testimony of nutrition scientists at its hearings and lobbying by individual nutritionists and nutrition groups. She characterises the change as moving from a 'selective' approach of nutrition directed at the poor to a 'universal' approach which addressed the problems of the wider population (Zebiche 1979).

The concept of overconsumption is especially relevant for modern industrial nations and central to this reconceptualisation of nutrition problems. The eminent nutritionist Jean Mayer, who chaired the first White House Conference on Food, Nutrition and Health in 1969 and also helped organise a commemorative conference two decades later, has described how he prepared for the first conference. He says he decided to look beyond poverty and include consumer concerns, partly because of the link between diet and chronic disease, but also because it had become clear to him that a 'reform effort' which addressed the perceived needs of the middle classes would draw more support and potentially benefit more people. Addressing consumer issues related to food was, he believed, another way to promote broader interest in nutrition (Mayer 1990:16). This calls to mind the work of Ellen Richards and W.O. Atwater. Again the interests of the middle class seem to have been the basis for establishing the importance of the scientist-reformers' agenda.

It is clear that there is an epidemiological justification for concern about heart disease in industrialised, affluent countries. It is just as clear that it was largely a political process that saw these health problems, in preference to others, become the central focus of Good Nutrition in the US from the late 1970s.

The redirection of attention from undernutrition to overconsumption and heart disease served a number of purposes. First, it increased the proportion of the population identified as having nutrition disorders. This point was intemperately expressed by McGovern himself when he introduced the National Nutrition Act to Congress in June 1975:

> Franklin Roosevelt spoke of the shameful fact that one-third of the Nation was malnourished. Today nearly the entire Nation misnourished (sic) because of the misuse of abundance. Tens of millions have the resources to buy sufficient food, but lack the knowledge to choose correctly. Too often we eat enough but we are not well fed.
>
> Many who are not hungry are the new misnourished.
>
> The new misnourished are the overweight who are overfilled with empty calories.
>
> The new misnourished consume too many processed foods and an unbalanced diet.

The new misnourished are most of us, most of our children, and too many of those who seem most healthy.

This new misnourishment requires a new program of nutrition education. This bill is a good beginning. It is the result of years of research and long hours of hearings and investigations. As Chairman of the Senate Select Committee on Nutrition and Human Needs, I have listened to the range of experts; I have heard the mounting evidence of national misnourishment:

By the time our healthiest sons are 20, their arteries are already infiltrated with fat deposits—and the problem has worsened in the last 20 years. (McGovern 1975)

McGovern did not mention the arteries of the nation's healthiest daughters.

The shift of focus to overconsumption also broadened the base of support for nutrition programs by addressing issues of interest to the middle class.

Although various expert bodies in a number of countries had produced reports detailing epidemiological relationships between diet and disease and made a range of dietary recommendations, none had the professional or public impact of the McGovern Committee. Its report was a spectacularly successful strategy to keep nutrition in the public arena in the US. Past programs, directed at the poor, had reached a stage where they could probably expand no further. The McGovern Committee gave Good Nutrition a new rationale by linking it with fatal and disabling diseases, reinforced the clinical nutrition research agenda and offered the possibility of reducing health care costs. Because the committee had reached its conclusions through a very public political process, its report was widely discussed and debated in the American mass media and in professional journals. It also had an important influence, at government level, on many other countries. By the mid 1980s, guidelines similar to those of the McGovern Committee had been developed, although not always adopted, by governments in New Zealand, Canada, the UK and France (Truswell 1983). In 1989, the head of the CSIRO Division of Human Nutrition in Adelaide, South Australia, said the McGovern Committee recommendations had paved the way to ' . . . the worldwide promulgation of Dietary Guidelines' (Nestel 1989).

Where did the US get the idea of guidelines? The first dietary guidelines were developed for Scandinavian countries and published in 1968. Truswell lists the practical recommendations contained in the Scandinavian goals, which recur in the guidelines subsequently adopted by other countries:

- that the calorie supply in the diet should be in many cases reduced to prevent overweight;
- that the total fat consumption should be reduced from the present round 40% to 25–35% of total calories;
- that use of saturated fat should be reduced and consumption of polyunsaturated fat simultaneously increased;
- that the consumption of sugar and sugar-containing products should be reduced;
- that one should increase consumption of vegetables, fruit, potatoes, skimmed milk, fish, lean meat, and cereal products. From the medical and nutritional standpoint it is essential to emphasise the importance of regular exercise habits from childhood for all individuals with mainly sedentary work. (quoted in Truswell 1987:1063)

Nothing remarkable here. However there is an important difference in the way these recommendations were developed, particularly in their rationale.

Truswell notes that the guidelines' developers were addressing changes in European lifestyles. Physical work had been reduced because of mechanisation, and calorie consumption in Sweden had declined. The concern was that now, with reduced food intake, people might not be getting enough vitamins and minerals. This concern was exacerbated by the knowledge that the average person was consuming 42 per cent of calories in the form of fat, compared with 19 per cent at the turn of the century. A diet with fewer calories and more fat was all the more unlikely to provide sufficient vitamins and minerals. Only after promoting a reduction in the proportion of fat-derived calories in the average diet did the Scandinavians adopt reduced total fat consumption and heart disease prevention as a policy issue. The fact that heart disease was seen as a secondary consideration has important implications for the contention that Good Nutrition reinforces cultural values.

> After calculating different diets, additional reasons were also put forward for the changes worked out. It was believed that this fat reduction might help to counteract a too high supply of calories. In view of the correlation between consumption of saturated fats and the frequency of atherosclerotic heart disease it might also help to prevent this disease especially if part of the saturated fat . . . were at the same time replaced by polyunsaturated fat. The reduction of sugar consumption, particularly in the form of confectionery, should further be a measure in the fight against dental caries. (Blix *et al* quoted in Truswell 1987:1063)

There are different ways of conveying the same recommendations. Like Margaret Mead before them, the Scandinavian experts regarded the reasons given for recommended dietary changes as important. To them, putting forward the needs of people whose diets were relatively low in calories was less controversial than other rationales, such as the dietary fat–atherosclerosis connection.

The Scandinavian guidelines are also interesting in that, like the McGovern Committee's original Dietary Goals, they are not government recommendations. In this case they were issued by medical professional organisations from a number of Scandinavian countries. A section headed 'Consequences of faulty diet' makes the priorities clear:

> The high frequency of obesity, particularly in individuals over 40 years of age, indicates that there is an over-consumption of calories. An over-consumption of this kind results not only in obesity but may also contribute to the onset of some illnesses or to complicating them. As examples may be mentioned cardiovascular diseases, diabetes, gallstones and diseases due to overstrain of the skeleton and joints.
>
> A diet largely consisting of fatty and sugary foods may have many adverse consequences. Today a large section of the population have such a low calorie requirement that they risk getting deficient quantities of important nutrients such as protein, mineral substances and vitamins. Investigations carried out in various parts of Scandinavia have shown that within population groups with a low calorie consumption such as old people, teenage girls and the chronically sick, the supply of such substances is unsatisfactory. The high frequency of anaemia in women has a connection with the low intake of iron in their diet.
>
> Many products with a high sugar content, particularly when eaten as snacks between meals, may increase the occurrence of tooth decay (caries).
>
> The importance of diet in causing atherosclerosis has been increasingly seriously considered in recent years. There is a close connection between the development of atherosclerotic cardiovascular diseases and the serum cholesterol level. Middle-aged men with a high serum cholesterol get atherosclerotic heart disease more often than those that have a low serum cholesterol value. People with a hereditary tendency towards an increase in the serum cholesterol not infrequently develop severe atherosclerosis as early as 30–40 years of age. In population groups with an average low serum cholesterol, atherosclerotic cardiovascular diseases are less common than in groups with high serum cholesterol levels. (quoted in Keys 1968:260)

The discussion moves on to the importance of saturated fatty acids and their effect on serum cholesterol, the association of diets high in fats with high prevalence of disease, and other factors that may be responsible for high serum cholesterol levels such as physical activity, high blood pressure and 'physical factors'. This section of the report concludes:

> Changes in the blood vessels caused by atherosclerosis often take place very early, although the symptoms of the disease seldom appear before early middle age or later. If we want to try and prevent the disease by means of a special diet, it should be introduced at an early stage and the change of diet should apply to the whole population. (quoted in Keys 1968:261)

The reasoning behind the Scandinavian approach to dietary guidelines is important. Within this framework, an education program aimed at persuading people to eat less fat would target primarily women and older people, society's 'small eaters', and coronary heart disease prevention would have a lower priority. The rationale given for reducing fat consumption might be different for young and middle-aged men (heart disease prevention) than for women and older people (a nutritionally adequate diet within a limited energy intake).

Why in the US did nutrition experts choose coronary disease as the focus for their dietary goals and guidelines? Why did Australia adopt the American dietary guidelines rather than the Scandinavian? The facts presented so far suggest:

1. The US guidelines were developed in a political rather than a scientific arena. The issues which became the basis for the guidelines were chosen to gain maximum media coverage and to provide some 'curry' for what were seen as passive professional nutrition groups. The political nature of the committee process made cultural beliefs a stronger influence than they might have been in less political circumstances. The scientific basis of the McGovern Committee report was thin; according to Truswell, 'the first edition was written by a group of politically interested activists with small knowledge of nutrition' (Truswell 1987:1064).

2. The American Heart Association had been developing dietary recommendations for a number of years, and the committee staff were thus able to combine their interests with those of a recognised medical group already working in the area of dietary reform.

3. Heart disease was a particularly salient issue for the decision makers of the era. There were no women on the McGovern Committee, and most nutrition scientists and cardiologists at that

time were middle-aged men. Many who testified at committee hearings were researchers working in the area of heart disease.

The Goals, and subsequently the Guidelines, focused on over-consumption partly for cultural reasons related to beliefs about self-control which are part of the common construction of responsible behaviour in Western societies and partly as a result of incorrectly equating overconsumption of fat with overconsumption of food. Food consumption data available in both the US and Australia do not indicate that the average diet contained too much food. In addition, the so-called 'epidemic of killer diseases', or at least the prevalence of coronary heart disease, had been on the wane (in both countries) for at least eight years before the McGovern Committee report was released. One of the leading figures in the US Food and Drug Administration later retreated from the 'epidemic' rationale for guidelines, noting that they were important not because there was an epidemic of ill-health but rather because their introduction could improve health (Miller & Stephenson 1985:743).

The form that dietary guidelines took in the US favoured high-profile, male-privileging health issues and was influenced by organisational interests, in particular those of the American Heart Association. Had the McGovern Committee retained the original Scandinavian emphasis, 'small-eating' women and older people, rather than men, would have been at the forefront of concern.

One result of Good Nutrition's shift of focus to heart disease prevention has been multi-million-dollar community intervention programs telling people that they should eat less fat to reduce their risk of heart disease. The success of such programs is logically measured by their effect on heart disease rates. This is very difficult to assess, however, not least because the chain of events from public education to heart disease is long, complex and tenuous. In any case, premenopausal women are unlikely to benefit in this way from reducing their fat consumption because their risk is low in the first place. Indeed, no community intervention has yet been clearly shown to have reduced heart disease, although some have produced small reductions in some community risk-factor levels. One of the best-evaluated and longest-running community diet–heart intervention programs, the Stanford Five-City Project, was unable to show a positive result at its six-year follow-up (Fortmann *et al.* 1993).Similarly, the Minnesota Heart Health Program, a 13-year research and demonstration project to reduce heart disease morbidity and mortality has produced disappointing results in blood cholesterol reduction (Leupker, Murray, Jacobs, Mittelmark *et al.* 1994).

It may be that what was needed in the first place was a program directed at the immediate needs of women and older people—one promoting good-quality basic food choices (nutrient-dense diets), which ironically is essentially the same outcome that the heart disease chauvinists seek. Programs addressing issues more relevant to these population groups may be more successful, for example how to lose weight while making healthy food choices, or how to make small, easy-to-prepare, nutritious meals for older couples or people living alone. How prosaic! Not at all the stuff of exciting media coverage, intense professional debate, life-saving interventions and large clinical research grants. More likely, as well, to build the careers of women home economists than male biomedical scientists.

Contemporary Good Nutrition, then, appears to reflect the interests of bureaucrats and powerful groups of biomedical experts rather than those of the community at large.

DIETARY GUIDELINES IN PRACTICE

In 1990, Michael Gibney published a critical examination of dietary guidelines. He did not wish to join the debate about the guidelines' impact on heart disease, but instead asked whether the guidelines were practical in everyday terms.

Guidelines are the qualitative form of quantitative goals. For example, the goal for dietary fibre in Australia is: 'To increase dietary fibre intake to 30 grams per day or more by the year 2000.' This is translated into the guideline: 'Eat more breads and cereals (preferably wholegrain) and vegetables and fruits.'

Similarly, the goal 'To reduce the contribution of fat to dietary energy from 38 per cent to 33 per cent or less by the year 2000' is translated into the guideline 'Avoid eating too much fat.'

When the actual diets of groups of people in Australia, the US and the UK are studied, very few of them are found to fulfil the recommendations in the guidelines (Black 1987, Gibney 1990, Harvey *et al.* 1990). This could be seen as a problem of people not 'complying' with the guidelines (Harvey *et al.* 1990), which is the most common interpretation of the gap between theory and practice. However, it is possible, rather than blaming the victim, to see the guidelines themselves as a problem. For example, applying the fibre goal becomes difficult when total energy intake is low. For older people and most women, eating 30g of fibre a day is unreal-

Percentage of the Victorian population achieving dietary targets

Percentages of people reaching single dietary targets

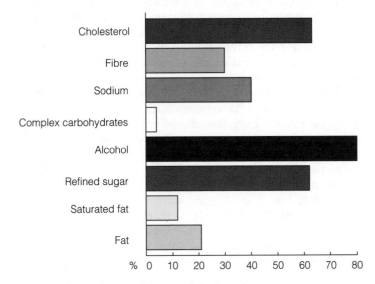

Percentages of people reaching multiple targets

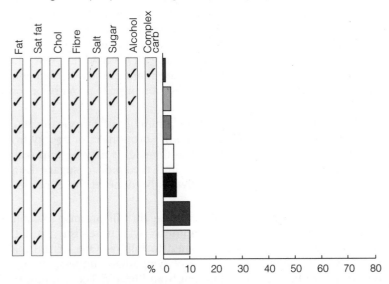

Source: K. Baghurst, 'The dietary seesaw', *Nutrition Issues and Abstracts* 4,
November 1994

istic; for children consuming less than 1000 kilocalories (kcal) a day it is 'clearly ridiculous' (Black 1987).

The messages of dietary guidelines can easily be misused and misinterpreted by both health workers and the community. Studies of the dietary changes made by individuals as a result of receiving dietary advice have revealed unpredictable and sometimes undesirable consequences. For example, the knowledge that some foods, such as dairy products or meat, contain relatively high levels of fat may lead people to reduce their consumption of these foods rather than choosing lower-fat versions such as lean meat or skimmed milk. One British study has shown that some people will reduce their milk consumption rather than drink low-fat milk. Popkin *et al.*'s data suggest another consequence, namely, that American women may be consuming more low-fat milk overall but less low-fat milk as individuals. In other words, more women are drinking low-fat milk, but in smaller amounts. If Good Nutrition campaigns are responsible for this shift, one might conclude that dietary guidelines have been good to the marketers of low fat milk but not to those concerned about the quality of women's food choices (Popkin *et al.* 1989).

If the same thing happens with meat, women may be at increased risk for two health problems related to undernutrition, namely osteoporosis and anaemia. People may shift (or not) to lower-fat products for a number of reasons, including taste, cost or the need to use different cooking methods. Today's dietary reformers are as much in the dark as Atkinson with his Aladdin oven when it comes to understanding the intricate ramifications of their interventions. 'Market research' is virtually nonexistent in nutrition programs.

Gibney has also pointed out for a number of European groups that if sugar consumption is reduced the proportion of energy from fat is raised, simply as a matter of arithmetic. It may be impossible to adhere to both the 'reduce fat' and the 'reduce sugar' dietary guidelines: keeping to one may always be done at the expense of the other.

This raises the ghost of Atwater yet again. His promise to control workers' social unrest through nutrition was unrealistic, and the strategies he proposed were doomed to failure. One of the main elements in that failure was a lack of sympathetic understanding of the everyday life of people different from himself. The promise that adherence to the dietary guidelines will reduce heart disease and health care costs may be similarly discredited, for comparable reasons. The advocates of scientific dietary reform often make the disclaimer that in public health one is forced to act without complete knowledge and that applying dietary guidelines may do good but will probably do no harm. This is said largely in ignorance of the often unforeseen effects of interventions on food choices and on everyday life.

Nutrition experts must question the likelihood that programs based on scientific dietary reform will achieve the health outcomes promised. This, Gibney says, is an important issue for those who teach the dietary guidelines in educational and community programs:

> [the] credibility of nutritionists and dietitians will diminish if the advice we offer is not effective, not feasible or not practicable; in other words poorly thought out . . . Nutrition and dietetics must not allow the field of epidemiology to dictate the pace of development of our subject such that we cease to be critical in our thinking and fail to see and appreciate the weaknesses in our own arguments. (Gibney 1990:253)

If history repeats itself, the biomedical advocates of scientific dietary reform—the modern-day Atwaters—will go back to their laboratories and continue their careers in a newer or more promising area. Oat bran, barley, fish oils, olive oil, calcium, sodium, garlic, anti-oxidants . . . the possibilities are legion. Even the coronary heart disease issue may become 'exhausted' and turn out not to have 'a very illustrious history', setting the stage for nutrition to be 'rescued' by something else.

Unfortunately, the education programs of the dietary guidelines era have been marked by an uncritical assumption that everyone should change their food choices. In contrast, the American nutrition educator Helen Guthrie has noted that most diets have their good points and that people need to know what they are doing well so they can identify which choices could be changed (Guthrie 1987:1396).

Dietary guidelines may represent the best and worst of what Good Nutrition can be about. They can focus and mobilise effort and resources, but they can also mislead, especially when their intent is an authoritarian style of social reform. Dietary guidelines have served to focus the efforts of the World Health Organization, health professionals, governments and food producers on a clear-cut set of rules. Truswell believes that this is preferable to the 'almost anarchy in public health nutrition in the 1970s' (Truswell 1987:1069). Guidelines have certainly found wide acceptance internationally among experts, government departments, and in some cases national and state governments.

Dietary guidelines rode into being on the back of a critique of the food group approach to Good Nutrition, but they may prove to be even more problematic than the system they replaced, partly because they have attracted so much support from scientists, governments, research-funding bodies and health promoters.

Good nutrition will always have some packaging, but it is vital that participation in the creation of the packaging be opened to a wider range of interests and that the nature of the packaging be explicit and open for discussion. In this way, inconsistencies can be debated outside the exclusive community of medical and nutrition experts.

6

Good Nutrition as a form of social control

Few spin the web of mystification, most just get caught. (Caplan 1988)

Good Nutrition is frequently, perhaps mostly, authoritarian. It teaches what to think, rather than how to think, about food and health. Community-wide dietary reform based on the epidemiological theory of Geoffrey Rose creates a dilemma for nutrition education. The strategy of risk factor reduction, including dietary change, theoretically will have great benefits for a population but promises little benefit to individuals. Women in particular are disadvantaged by this approach, because the results of studies of men have inappropriately been applied to them. Dietary reform advocates have also privileged expert knowledge over domestic and household perspectives. Women are seen as responsible for nutrition in the home, but the influence of men on family food choices remains unrecognised, and in terms of coronary heart disease, the wife is still viewed as responsible for her husband's illness. Because of all this and, perhaps most importantly, because in our society eating is inextricably tied to women's appearance and their social roles, Good Nutrition is easily used to exert pressure on women.

It is not necessary to resort to a conspiracy theory to understand how contemporary Good Nutrition programs can be a source of social control. Social control is exercised by any social institution which attempts to ensure that people follow the rules it sees as acceptable. In these terms, the church, the law and medicine all qualify as sources of social control. John and Barbara Ehrenreich have noted that they are not concerned that the medical system functions in the way it does. Rather, they are concerned about the content of the social control it exercises. They also note that medical management of, for example, childbirth and human relationships can be seen as co-optative control, that is, as enlarging the purview of medicine to cover more and more aspects of everyday life. They are interested in what impact this control has on people's lives (Ehrenreich & Ehrenreich 1978:49).

Geoffrey Rose has developed the idea that affluent societies are composed of 'sick populations', that is, by extension, all Australians are patients in need of dietary reform. The Ehrenreichs' question in this context then becomes: What effect does the professional management of eating have on people's lives, that is, on their beliefs, self-image, and work and family roles?

The social control function of Good Nutrition is problematic and could be unjustifiable if, for example, it disadvantaged many in advantaging a few. Good Nutrition programs based on the dietary guidelines are a concern in these terms. The intention behind the 'population strategy' for preventing heart disease through diet is ultimately to alter society's norms of behaviour and to influence what are deemed socially acceptable food choices.

There are no particular groupings or organisations with a deliberate game plan to control others. However, there is a clear gap between the available evidence of benefit (not much) and the extent of the action which has already been taken in persuasive Good Nutrition campaigns. An understanding of contemporary Good Nutrition needs to include both a critique of the scientific rationale of Good Nutrition and an examination of its less rational elements.

Naomi Wolf calls our society's beliefs about beauty and women 'necessary fictions' which society tells itself (Wolf 1990:6). It is likely that some 'necessary fictions' have adhered to science as it has come to dominate food choice advice. Science has yet to find, much less illuminate, many of nutrition's darker corners. Two which need to be dealt with are the authoritarian nature of Good Nutrition, which allows program planners to assume that they know best what people should eat while keeping private uncertainties about their recommendations, and the integration of sexist assumptions into Good Nutrition programs—particularly those related to coronary disease prevention.

GOOD NUTRITION AS AUTHORITARIAN

Dietary guidelines are intended to make their impact on health at the population level rather than at the individual level. When dietary guidelines are promoted to reduce cardiovascular disease rates, programs based on them are subject to what the epidemiologist Geoffrey Rose has termed 'the prevention paradox', namely that: 'A preventive measure which brings much benefit to the population offers little to each participating individual' (Rose 1985:38). This paradox arises from what some have called the 'mass population approach' to prevention of coronary heart disease.

> The mass population approach seeks to reduce the risk factors prevailing in the whole population by encouraging and enabling appropriate dietary changes, cessation of cigarette smoking, uptake of exercise and so on. The basis of this approach is that the great majority of CHD cases are found amongst those whose risk factors are only moderately raised or average. Proponents argue that relatively small reductions in mean population blood cholesterol level can result in many more CHD cases prevented. (Davis 1987:7)

The obverse of this approach is that although Good Nutrition programs seek to persuade everyone to change their food choices, relatively few people will avoid a heart attack because of dietary change, some people will have a heart attack despite dietary change, and many people will not change their food choices and not have a heart attack. Moreover, there is no way of determining who benefited from the program and who did not. Davison *et al.* have called these 'anomalous deaths and unwarranted survivals' (Davison *et al.* 1991:16). Those who develop and carry out Good Nutrition programs have not yet found a way to come to grips with these realities, much less to explain them to the community.

Perhaps the one program which retained some honesty in this respect was the North Karelia Project conducted in Finland during the 1970s. According to the organisers:

> As a whole, the aim was to inspire 'community action for change' in which people would participate not necessarily for their own sake but for the sake of North Karelia and the Project . . . thus emphasising incentives other than those related to their long-term disease risk (Puska *et al.* 1985:159).

The value of the mass population strategy is expressed in population statistics, and it is impossible for individuals to know whether they will benefit from dietary change. This raises questions about both the ethics and the effectiveness of Good Nutrition programs based on these ideas.

There is a very important difference between preventing a heart attack and reducing the risk of having one. This is particularly so if the reduction is small and the risk was small to start with, as, for example, in the case of premenopausal women. But this is not how dietary guidelines are usually 'sold' to individuals or the community, as Davison and his colleagues note:

> Rather than communicate the paradoxical nature of population strat-egies to the general public, the response of health educators and health promoters . . . has been to disseminate simple messages sug-gesting that 'saturated fat is bad for you—eat less', 'obesity is danger-ous—stay slim', 'exercise is good for you—do more' etc. The strong implication that flows from the contemporary 'health lifestyles' move-ment is that, for example, all saturated fat is always bad for everyone. The fact that this type of message is at best a distortion of the epidemiological evidence appears not to have diminished the zeal of its delivery. (Davison *et al.* 1991:16)

These authors call this 'a worthy dishonesty' based on two assumptions health promoters make, first that people will not respond to campaign persuasion unless they think they will benefit personally and second

> that the broadcasting of propaganda based on half-truth, simplification and distortion is a legitimate use of public funds, so long as the goal of the enterprise is the good of the community. (Davison *et al.* 1991:16–17)

Essentially such programs are caught within the set of problems that arise from adopting an ethic of attitude rather than an ethic of responsibility. With Peter Berger, I believe that it is not enough to have intended good. Responsibility must be taken for consequences whatever they are.

A typical reason for proceeding with such programs in the absence of a greater degree of certainty that they can reduce death and illness from coronary heart disease was that given by Dr Mark Hegsted when he announced the release of the American Dietary Goals in 1977. His justification for promoting dietary reform was a sense of obligation and responsibility to inform the public about up-to-date knowledge and assist them to make what he saw as 'correct food choices' (quoted in Austin & Hitt 1979:339).

Variants on this theme have been put forward on numerous occasions since the American Goals were launched, but to this day no data from community-wide coronary disease risk-factor reduction programs have decisively demonstrated that the mass population approach works as Geoffrey Rose and others have predicted. Studies of some community programs, such as the Stanford Five-City study, have shown a reduction in risk factors but not in death or illness from coronary disease (Farquhar *et al.* 1990). A later evaluation of the same program has been able to demonstrate only changes in women's knowledge and none in risk factors (Fortmann *et al.* 1993). There is not yet an accumulation of knowledge anywhere near sufficient to inspire confidence in the practicality or the efficacy of community-wide dietary reform programs aimed at reducing death and illness from coronary disease.

Zola emphasises the rights of people who are advised to follow medical advice, saying that regardless of the promised benefits, consumers are entitled to query the relevance of those benefits and to ask who decides which benefits are selected for promotion in the community (Zola 1972). Similar questioning of contemporary Good Nutrition is denied to the community. Dietary guidelines thus have the potential to develop into a problematic, potentially damaging form of orthodoxy.

Researchers working in the area covered by one of the best-known community intervention projects, Heartbeat Wales, have identified important and ironical outcomes of the perception of being at increased risk of heart disease. When 'anomalous deaths and unwarranted survivals' become more obvious in the community, that is when 'the last person' you would expect to have a heart attack has one and the people who do not adopt the recommended behaviour do not succumb to the threatened result, the result is that 'fatalistic cultural concepts are given more rather than less explanatory power' despite the intention to achieve the reverse (Davison *et al.* 1991:16).

Within hospitals, 'blaming the victim' must cause distress to many heart attack patients and their families. When a 33-year-old colleague of Dr Paul Marantz died after a heart attack (an 'unwarranted death' in the terms of Davison *et al.*), a medical co-worker told Marantz that he was a 'real couch potato'—despite his lack of classic risk factors for a heart attack. The incident prompted Marantz to write to the *American Journal of Public Health*. He says with some feeling that when epidemiological explanations are applied to individuals they may be 'terribly unfair' and goes on, 'A patient with acute cardiac disease will experience anxiety, fear, and the loss of control; we run the risk of adding to this a feeling of responsibility, guilt, and remorse' (Marantz 1990:1186).

At the level of the individual doctor–patient relationship, Marantz says doctors could resolve the conflict between individual experience and the mass population approach by advising their patients to modify their risk factors while 'helping them understand that there is no life-style, no matter how hedonistic, which assures disease; just as there is no life-style, no matter how austere, which assures longevity' (Marantz 1990:1187).

This humane approach seems in stark contrast to the use of feelings of guilt, remorse and responsibility to achieve dietary behaviour change in the community.

Davison *et al.* see the problem as being a conflict between self-interest and shared values. Should the point of persuasion be that people are asked to change their behaviour for the good of the community, rather than themselves as individuals, as in the North Karelia Project? They propose that a solution to the problems of the prevention paradox will only come when health is seen as a collective rather than an individual phenomenon.

WOMEN, GOOD NUTRITION AND SOCIAL CONTROL

Lesley Doyal, in *The Political Economy of Health*, points out that as its cruder forms are removed, sexism will remain in some areas but in a subtler form, especially in the field of health care. As medicine has taken over responsibilities in more and more areas of everyday life, women in particular have come into more frequent contact with doctors and the medical system. Doctors now claim special knowledge in child rearing and female reproduction, including conception and contraception as well as childbirth. The recent debate on the role of medicine in the recasting of menopause as an illness and the widespread use of hormone replacement therapy is another example. Women visit doctors more frequently than men and their emotional distress is likely to be treated by a doctor. As Doyal observes, the expansion of medicine's sphere of influence, which is the basis for its role in social control, has had more of an impact on women's lives than on men's. It may be more difficult to identify medicine's mechanisms of social control because they are associated with sources of help. Thus it becomes important to recognise the more subtle forms of social control that medicine exerts on women (Doyal 1979:218).

Food obviously has intimate ties with women's roles in society. This, together with Good Nutrition's shift to a more medical, disease-focused orientation, makes it particularly important to scrutinise Good Nutrition for these subtle kinds of control.

One of the more disturbing aspects of the whole picture of

coronary disease prevention is the lack of differentiation between men and women when the effect of risk factors on disease development or the outcomes of treatments and preventive strategies are discussed. This imbalance has recently come under scrutiny.

The US Congressional Caucus on Women's Issues has asked the country's major research-funding bodies whether they consider balanced gender representation in research studies when assessing grant applications. As the *Journal of the American Medical Association* remarked when reporting this: 'Efforts to streamline studies by using the most homogeneous population possible have filled medical libraries with data on middle-aged white men. Even female rats are commonly excluded from basic research' (Cotton 1990:1049–1050, 1055).

Because the risk of premature death from heart disease is greatest for middle-aged men, this group will benefit most from successful prevention programs. Premenopausal women, because their risk is very low, will benefit much less. Yet because of their role in family food management and their greater likelihood of actually changing their behaviour, it is women who are affected most by Good Nutrition programs. Indeed many, perhaps most Good Nutrition programs deliberately target women because they are seen as responsible for family food choices.

The basic medical research examining the effect of diet on serum cholesterol levels and the relationship between cholesterol and coronary heart disease has been carried out on men and the results extrapolated to women. So, for example, a Western Australian campaign to increase community awareness of the need to reduce fat intake was directed at 'people aged 20–40 years, who make decisions about their own or their family's food choices' (Brown 1988:47; Miller *et al.* 1987). It would probably have been more honest to say 'women' rather than 'people'.

Although these issues have been raised recently (O'Dea 1991), the essential nature of the dietary guidelines for Australians has remained unchanged in the 1992 revision. Although the amended guidelines recognise two nutrition issues, iron-deficiency anaemia and osteoporosis, which particularly concern women, this only reinforces the guidelines' orientation to women generally. The question of whether it is wise to subsume women in a blanket recommendation to adopt heart-disease prevention diets remains unaddressed.

WOMEN AS 'GATEKEEPERS'

The tenor and approach of nutrition education suggest that women have the control and decision making responsibility needed to easily change their family's diet. Nutrition has adopted the term 'gatekeeper', first used in the 1940s by social psychologist Kurt Lewin, to describe the role of women in the flow of food into the home. Lewin's idea is summarised by McIntosh and Zey:

> Food gets onto the table through what [Lewin] calls 'channels' such as the grocery store, the garden and the refrigerator. The selection of channels and the food which travels through them is under the control of the gatekeeper. (McIntosh & Zey 1989:319)

These authors use a study of the literature on power in families to show how much more complicated are the dynamics of families and food than Lewin assumes. In particular, they note that in more traditional families, the husband's control of the purse strings and women's obligations to produce a harmonious family life, bring the gatekeeper concept into question. Charles and Kerr have also questioned this idea in terms of its relationship to health education. Central to their analysis is the concept of women 'privileging' their husband's food preferences and both women's and men's views on 'proper food for a man': 'Because food plays such an important role in the marital relationship, and regular provision of proper meals for men is a fundamental part of being a proper wife and mother, women are constrained by their partners' preferences' (Charles & Kerr 1986:71).

These authors argue that nutrition education should also target men, that boys too should learn about nutrition in school, and that those who would change family food choices should seek to alter the food environment. They are concerned about the impact that nutrition education may have on women: 'the message is clear that targeting women alone with health education will only serve to increase their burden of guilt rather than lead to a transformation of family eating habits' (Charles & Kerr 1986:72).

Carole Counihan (1988), an anthropologist, has written about the traditional roles of Florentine women and the influence of social change on their lives. These women traditionally had influence and prestige in their families although not outside them. Their part of this bargain was to serve others before themselves and to run their households with skill and concern for the needs of other family members, especially their husbands and sons—in short, to be 'good women'. The younger women Counihan spoke to were more likely

The conflicts of women's domestic service

Source: J. Horacek, *Life on the Edge,* Spinifex, Melbourne, 1992

to be better educated, to work in paid employment for both personal satisfaction and out of financial need, and to find conflict between their role outside the home and Florentine women's traditional domestic role. They felt much more independent than their mothers and related this to having their own money. They relied more on others for childcare and food preparation, thought it unjust that men had not changed their roles as the recipients of women's ministrations, and felt guilty that they could not maintain their mothers' standards of domestic management and food preparation. Counihan's portrait brings out the essential conflict of contemporary women in all industrialised, consumer-oriented countries. Traditionally, satisfaction and recognition have been bought at the cost of

73

dependence on men. Today, independence is bought at the cost of guilt and the rigours of the second shift.

Andrea and Tony Worsley (1988) found, in their study of families in Adelaide, South Australia, that redistribution of traditional domestic responsibilities is 'minor' in households where the woman works outside the home. In the families they studied, men were still cast as breadwinners and women as homemakers even where both partners had paid jobs. They report that this is consistent with international findings.

What should be made of this? The question of who makes decisions about what food is served in families is a very complex one. Nutrition experts should think critically about their expectations of women in families. If the gatekeeper concept is influencing their interpretation of nutrition data and program planning, they should be aware of that concept's 'hidden curriculum'—the notion of the 'good woman'—and of its potential both to disadvantage women and to mislead program planners.

A recent editorial in the *Medical Journal of Australia* which discussed the impact of a 'caring spouse' on men's heart attack rates had it that

> a caring spouse often is supportive in the development of the contin-
> uation of healthy habits and with continued compliance with advice
> and medication in those who are already known to have coronary
> heart disease. Wives remain the usual suppliers of meals within house-
> holds and often are the major influence on behaviours in the home.
> (Goble 1989:184)

Such views, which allocate responsibility for family health to women, do not recognise the complexities of family interaction and the importance of non-nutritional risk factors and behaviours. Rather, they are based on cultural beliefs or perhaps wishful thinking about what women 'should do' in the home.

NUTRITION EDUCATION'S HIDDEN CURRICULUM

Just as problematic assumptions may underlie nutrition's expecta-
tions of women, they may also underlie the content of Good Nutrition. Experts have been telling women how to meet their family responsibilities for years. Ehrenreich and English show how advice to women may be laced with cultural messages. They point out that in the US after the turn of the century, domestic science instruction represented an effort to discipline and Americanise the poor. 'The

useful information—on cooking, shopping, etc.—. . .necessarily came packaged with the entire ideology of "right living". And right living meant living like the American middle class lived, or aspired to live' (Ehrenreich & English 1978:156).

Good Nutrition has always been a package deal, nutrition science wrapped in contemporary (sexist) ideology, which takes a rather romantic view of women's role in families and denies patriarchal aspects of family life.

VIEWS OF WOMEN

Views of women in Western medical textbooks have been shown to be inaccurate and pejorative. Glenda Katroulis, writing about gynaecology texts used in Australian medical schools, refers to the 'hidden curriculum', that is the attitudes and assumptions which influence medical practice. These attitudes are often disguised as science. The student learns not only gynaecology, for instance, but a certain view of women. Two of the issues on which the women's health movement has challenged medical orthodoxy are the way doctors and the health system view women and the consequences which can arise from this view.

Ehrenreich and English remarked in 1973 that medicine's main contribution to sexism was to portray women as both sick and sickening to men. These notions seem to retain currency today. A 1988 publication of the Australian Institute of Health lists menopause as an illness along with sexually transmitted diseases, menstrual problems and vaginal infections. In 1989 the *Medical Journal of Australia* published an article titled 'Marriage is associated with a lower risk of ischaemic heart disease in men' (Malcolm *et al.* 1989) together with a commentary titled 'Do caring wives protect against cardiac disease?' (Goble 1989). The article interpreted higher mortality rates in single men, as evidence that wives have a protective effect on their husbands. This view of women as responsible for men's health appears to be the corollary of their portrayal as potentially sickening to men.

Numerous aspects of women's lives, from their educational attainments to their 'caring' qualities, have been examined to explain their husband's heart disease (or lack of it). There has been no such examination of ways in which men might influence their wives' heart disease (or lack of it). On the contrary, the *MJA* commentary mentioned above observed: 'The wife's death as a result of coronary heart disease becomes a marker of the surviving husband's risk of a coronary death' (Goble 1989). At least four papers have come from the Framingham Study examining the relationship of aspects of wives' behaviour, social status, level of education and employment status on their husbands' heart disease. After the publication of one such paper which reported an increased heart attack rate in husbands with less education than their wives, a popular health magazine reported the results on the front page under the heading 'Your wife could be killing you':

> If your wife works, she could well be slowly killing you. Husbands of wives involved in high-level business have lower self-esteem and higher rates of heart attack. The Framingham Heart Study results were amazing. Men married to women with university or college educations were almost three times as likely to have a heart attack. To have this effect the women had to have worked outside the home for more than half of their married lives. The extent and type of tertiary education was also important. Men married to women in white-collar occupations have the highest risk. They were three to five times more likely to have a heart attack than men married to women in clerical positions. (*Health '84* June 1984)

Another study based on Framingham data whose results were published in 1980 sought to establish whether the increase in the number of women in paid work had led to an increase in their rates of coronary heart disease. The researchers found that the women most at risk of having a heart attack were clerical workers whose husbands were blue-collar workers and who had three or more children. They noted that these women's rate of coronary heart disease was almost twice that of male clerical workers. The researchers failed to explore the social and educational characteristics of these women's husbands or to theorise about how the husbands' behaviour might affect their wives' health. Moreover, the factors thought to affect men's heart disease (such as education level, Type A behaviour, smoking and so on) continue to be studied in relation to women's heart disease (Mathews *et al.* 1989). It is perhaps noteworthy that both the authors of a paper titled 'Is an educated wife hazardous to your health?' are women (Suarez and Barret-Connor 1984). They conclude that she is. They might have titled their paper 'Is your education making your husband sick?' but chose instead to address it to men. The authors subsequently noted that they 'were not happy with the public health implications' of their findings but they did not give details of their misgivings (Suarez & Barret-Connor 1985).

There seems to be good reason to believe that the prejudice against women as sickening to men is still operative in both expert and community discourse on coronary heart disease. As Spitzer and Rodin have shown of eating-behaviour research related to obesity, community beliefs are represented in researchers' work and can help shape the questions they ask. They call this researchers exercising their 'layman's intuition'. Behavioural researchers sought to identify an 'obese eating style', probably based on the notion that the obese are gluttons. Experiments tried unsuccessfully to establish that overweight people ate differently from people of normal weight or that they engaged in 'greedy' behaviour such as eating quickly, taking larger mouthfuls, or eating secretly.

Traditional moral beliefs can become integrated into research goals. The exploration of how the women's characteristics are related to their husbands' heart attacks is an example of this phenomenon. In accepting, or at least not actively questioning, these dubious ideas, those who would change women's behaviour can exercise a potent form of social control by implying that they are responsible for both causing and preventing their husbands' heart attacks. Thus women may accept responsibility not only for their own heart disease but for their partners' as well.

WOMEN AND THE PREVENTION OF
HEART DISEASE THROUGH DIET

How are we to view Scott Grundy's recent statement that no clinical trials have been carried out to establish whether lowering serum cholesterol levels benefits women? The benefits of the community-wide application of dietary guidelines are still uncertain, particularly for older men and for women (Grundy 1990; McCormick & Skrabanek 1988). Nutrition policymakers' dictum that 'we should act now even though all the evidence is not in' could perhaps be more frankly rephrased to add 'especially for women and older men'. As Crouse has pointed out (1990), current nutrition advice may even be harmful to women, since by adopting low-fat diets they may be lowering their blood levels of protective cholesterol. Why is this not a point of discussion, much less debate in contemporary Good Nutrition or its community interventions? Whose interests are being served by the current designation of issues as debatable or not? Women's interests seem to have been assigned lower priority than either men's or the community's, if indeed they have been considered separately at all. What is more likely is that, as in other areas of patriarchal society, women's interests are subsumed by those of men. It is assumed that what is beneficial for men is also good for women.

WOMEN AND WEIGHT CONTROL

The current Australian guideline on weight control is likely to receive more emphasis in the future, given the resurgence of interest in this area. Again, sexist beliefs about women's appearance make this guideline particularly susceptible to misuse and to unintended harm for women. Female eating disorders have received considerable attention in the medical literature in the past decade. At the same time a sizeable literature has grown up chronicling women's own experiences, one of the earliest and best-known examples being Susie Orbach's *Fat is a Feminist Issue* (1978). More books have followed, many of them written by women who have suffered from eating difficulties themselves. However, Good Nutrition programs seem to have been reluctant to grapple with the dilemma of how to address the medical problem of overweight while at the same time dealing with the undeniable risks for women posed by programs which lock into what Naomi Wolf (1990) has called 'the beauty myth'.

One of the most important of Wolf's targets is the way in which the pursuit of beauty controls women's behaviour and reduces their potential for achieving power. The beauty myth may be the ultimate form of social control of women, and weight management advice, legitimised by medicine and health promotion programs, feeds and fuels it. Walden, in his historical treatment of concern about overweight, has shown that until the twentieth century, 'body moulding' was achieved by 'external compression' of one kind or another. The modern concern with 'naturalness', however, meant that women had to lose weight if they wanted to look fashionable. Body control thus 'becomes an expression of social control' (Walden 1985:364). Foreshadowing Wolf, Walden says:

> If females were going to upset society by being more open about sexuality and more demanding of their rights, control could be maintained by idealizing physical features which were difficult to retain . . . Much of their potential would be dissipated fretting about shortcomings, much of their energy would be invested trying to overcome them. Those who did conform to the ideal always would be conscious that

their advantages were inexorably slipping away. Besides, good looks would normally be possessed most fully at an age when they could be used least effectively. And as they faded, the pressure to diet and exercise would mount. It is not surprising that losing weight came to be primarily a female activity. (Walden 1985:365)

In a 1988 study of South Australian women, 43 per cent of the sample were found to be dieting for weight loss. Of these women, 60 per cent were overweight but 34 per cent were not (Crawford and Worsley 1988). Of a range of motivations suggested to the dieting women, 75 per cent wanted to 'feel better', 65 per cent wanted to 'look better' and 13 per cent were dieting to please a partner. In a society where, it seems, at any given time almost half of all adult females are dieting, 15 per cent of women are underweight and 20 per cent of women aged between 20 and 24 are underweight (National Heart Foundation 1989:47). Yet the mass media emphasise the health risks of being overweight, often using graphic 'danger messages'. Medical scientists are often quoted in these items. The release of the National Heart Foundation's Risk Factor Study, which showed an increase in obesity rates particularly among women, was reported in the press with statements like, 'The increasing number of Australians eating themselves to death has prompted the formation of an Australia-wide study group' and (under the headline 'Chewing our own graves') 'Australians are digging their graves with their teeth according to a Melbourne specialist pushing for a concerted effort to beat obesity' (*Geelong Advertiser* 1991).

Although the specialist referred to may not actually have used those words, the fear-inducing potential of such a report is obvious. The comment, in the same article, that 'the public had to realise the importance of excessive weight's impact on health' probably did not refer to the mental and physical health consequences of distress about being or becoming overweight. In a report in the *Sunday Age*, however, one expert was quoted as saying, in relation to the increased rates of obesity in post-menopausal women, that social factors were involved, that there might be a problem with the way overweight women were regarded by society, and that this problem should be addressed. The same commentator speculates that weight gain in later life is related to the relaxation of pressures on younger women to be slim (Stone 1991).

This fascinating notion appears to be a corollary of the theory that the desire to be seen as attractive controls women's weight when they are young. Older women, so the thinking seems to go, are perceived by society as less attractive and as a result 'let themselves go' when the pressure 'comes off'. This theory is supported by the authors of the editorial which accompanied the article by Crawford and Worsley:

> After puberty the energy needs of young women decrease, and it may be hypothesized that to maintain a 'normal weight' young women have to learn to control their body weight and hence to modify their eating habits and exercise patterns. The article by Crawford and Worsley in this issue of the *Journal* suggests that many Australian women do not achieve such control in adult life. (Abraham & Mira 1988:324)

These views too contain sexist values. Based on the available data, the following makes equally good sense:

> After puberty the energy needs of young men decrease, and it may be hypothesized that to maintain a normal weight young men have to learn to control their body weight and hence to modify their eating habits and exercise patterns. The NHF Risk Factor Study suggests that many Australian men do not achieve such control in either youth or adult life.

But the NHF study shows that at age 20 to 24, 25 per cent of men and 17 per cent of women are overweight or obese; among those aged 45 and over, 60 per cent of men and between 30 per cent and 57 per cent of women are in this category. In all age groups, the proportion of men who are overweight or obese is greater than that of women in the same category. The notion that young women need to control themselves in some way that young men do not, is part of the ideology of social control that can co-opt Good Nutrition.

As Abraham and Mira and Crawford and Worsley point out, educational and public health programs which try to get people to lose weight have the potential to create important problems:

> there is no use in bombarding a young woman who is weight and shape conscious, but who is eating a sensible diet, with information that is aimed at a middle-aged, obese politician or public servant [both of whom, of course, may be women]. (Abraham & Mira 1988: 324)

Given the negative views held about the overweight in affluent societies, it would be undesirable to 'bombard' obese politicians and public servants of either sex, but given the particularly oppressive nature of society's demands on women to 'look good', such a bombardment is likely to affect women's self-esteem and public worth more adversely.

In Victoria, Australia, a spate of political cartoons targeting the state's first woman premier, Joan Kirner, sparked a debate over whether she was being treated differently, that is more unfairly, because she was overweight. One view was that she couldn't 'take it like a man' (and should have been able to). But there is little doubt that derisory remarks about appearance, particularly body weight and shape, carry a different meaning when a woman is the target. Such remarks are generally seen as more derogatory and more likely to undermine the confidence and sense of self-worth of women than of men. Society selects carefully the areas in which it will champion equal opportunity.

At a press conference for International Women's Day in 1991, Joan Kirner was reported as saying she did not think she was portrayed unfairly by the media but 'What I do say is, women are still judged in different terms in the media than men.' It was rare, she said, for the media to comment on male cabinet ministers' suits, what they had for breakfast or whether they were on a diet. 'And yet for women, their shape, their clothes, the fact that they may not be quite the image that some media may want to portray them is still an issue. I think women in political life or public life ought to be judged on their contribution and not their personal image' (*Geelong Advertiser* 1991a).

How to prepare public education programs to address legitimate health concerns about overweight without at the same time exacerbating the problems which stem from cultural and social evaluations of bodies, especially women's bodies, is a problem that has yet to be widely discussed. The Victorian Health Promotion Foundation, a body funded through a tax on tobacco consumption, has started work in this area. It faces a difficult task, and will need to address fundamental views of society about women and of women about themselves.

OVERCONSUMPTION AS A NECESSARY FICTION

In Australia, a number of documents which set out the rationale for contemporary Good Nutrition have identified overconsumption of food as a cause for concern. The National Health and Medical Research Council (NHMRC) publication *Implementing the Dietary Guidelines for Australians* notes: 'By the late 1970s, however, it had become clear that the major nutritional problems in Australia related to overconsumption and not to underconsumption of foods' (1989:21). The *Health for All Australians* report by the Health

Targets and Implementation Committee states: 'The major nutritional problem in Australia is over-consumption of foods, aggravated by the sedentary lifestyle of many Australians.'

There is no evidence that Australians are eating more food than they did either before the turn of the century or just after the Second World War. Indeed, the indications are that they are consuming fewer calories. This too can lead to weight gain if energy expenditure has decreased even more. This latter possibility is a respectable speculation, while the first (that Australians might be eating more) is quite disreputable in scientific terms. Why has the anxiety about eating too much remained on the Good Nutrition agenda? It may well be that this concern is based less on facts than on traditional cultural fears, and that these fears call forth the sort of controlling strategies that were necessary when people were dependent on self-sufficiency in agriculture.

A number of authors have pointed out that historically, concerns about overindulgence in food tends to rise during periods of social disruption. Anxiety about control is sometimes also linked with the idea that disease is caused by 'civilisation' and its suppression of 'natural' behaviour. Walden offers what he sees as a speculative interpretation of these associations from medieval times through the Renaissance to more recent times (Walden 1985). He and other writers have suggested that the reason the ruling classes introduced sumptuary laws was to limit the celebration of the body (among other things) by the non-aristocratic, newly rich merchant class. When spending was curtailed, youth gave one a natural advantage. Thus it became highly prized.

> The aesthetic of youth was inherently attractive as a device for class domination in the economic and social situation of well-to-do families . . . As class and background got obscured, physical appearance became correspondingly more important as an indicator of status and respectability. (Walden 1985: 354–355)

Walden argues that industrialisation further boosted the value of youth, which was associated with strength, cheap labour costs and educability. As youth became more highly valued, so did being slim.

During this period, people began to worry more about materialism and overconsumption and the need to promote what was considered to be natural. These concerns extended to food. Discussing dietary regimes such as those promoted by Cheyne, a seventeenth century English physician, Bryan Turner says they con-

82

trasted the frugality of nature with the excesses of civilisation (Turner 1982).

As early as the eighteenth century, medical experts were linking the notion of diseases of civilisation with overconsumption and overindulgence (Turner 1982). They viewed obesity as not only a physiological problem but also a sign of moral deviance (Turner 1982:268). In traditional terms, of course, gluttony is one of the seven deadly sins and the only one which confesses itself. Like modern Good Nutrition, these attitudes express concerns about self-control and conservation in beliefs about appropriate food choices.

To assert that Good Nutrition is a cultural invention does not necessarily invalidate its scientific precursors. Culture and science each have their place. The problem is that their fusion, as in the case of Good Nutrition, can give rise to an entity with a life of its own. This product is rarely recognised by scientists or health educators as a transformation of nutrition research, distinct from the research itself.

Good Nutrition will have to be seen as more than dietary guidelines if women's health is to be supported and enhanced in the 1990s and beyond. Women, men and children must no longer be regarded as populations to be changed in the quest for impersonal and imposed goals without reference to the realities of everyday life.

7

The subversive nature of everyday life

 Many nutrition experts see everyday life as a nuisance, a context in which people behave badly and a barrier to program plans. It is something they try to understand if they have to, but only insofar as it can be overcome to meet broader goals. Lay people, however, have their own view of the world, which includes views on food choices and health behaviours. They are more likely to make changes to these areas on their own, rather than experts' terms.

Examples of how the insider view differs from the outsider's include middle-class families' views of health-promoting behaviours, members of ethnic groups adapting their food choices to the dominant culture, children's consumption of lollies, and the preferences of adults who depend on others to feed them. All these groups strategise to fulfil their preferences. Even where people are subordinate to others—children to their parents, institutionalised people to rules, and women to men's food preferences, they actively seek to get their own food needs met.

Similarly, a 'lay epidemiology' exists concerning who has heart attacks and why, and it is at odds with the views of the experts. Non-experts know people who have had a heart attack but did not 'break the rules'. They also know people who smoke and are overweight yet do not succumb. This produces a sense of distance between expert advice and the realities of everyday life.

Also, what is presented as expert knowledge may be biased and selectively reported. Technically expert nutrition knowledge may not necessarily be more worthy as a basis of nutrition programs than lay perceptions; nor are all experts necessarily equally expert at formulating policy or deciding how their expertise should be used. There is, therefore, a case for reviewing the relative roles of expert and everyday knowledge in shaping Good Nutrition.

Some of these dilemmas are demonstrated by the limitations of consensus development conferences. If more studies were done of medical and nutrition experts and how they use their knowledge to meet their own goals, the consequence might be a better understanding both of the issues involved and of how experts create the gap between the application of their knowledge and the realities of everyday life.

THE IDEAL VERSUS THE REAL

One of the most frequently discussed problems of dietary research is how to be sure that the information collected represents what people actually eat. How sure can the researchers be that people do what they say they do? Everyday life is a problem for nutrition researchers, and especially for scientific diet reform, because it brings into play the idiosyncratic, the unexpected and the unpredictable. When a person says, 'I have three vegetables with a hot dinner at night,' this probably represents the ideal situation. The real one might go more like this: 'I like to have three vegetables with a hot meal at night because I think I should and I try to because I know it's important to eat enough fibre, but sometimes I work late and buy something on the way home. And usually on Tuesdays I play squash with Hugh and we go to McDonald's after, and last week the freezer broke down and so I only had potatoes. When I have visitors I always do spaghetti because I make a fabulous Bolognese sauce. Hugh loves broccoli and I can't stand it, so when broccoli's on the menu, which is too often, I don't eat it.'

While some researchers find everyday life a problem (it has a tendency to complicate numerical calculations in nutrition), it could be considered the most interesting and the most human of nutrition's many faces. Indeed, to truly understand the implications of Good Nutrition programs, an appreciation of the human face of nutrition is essential. If everyday life is considered a nuisance and people adapting to it are seen as less than responsible, this says more about the experts holding those views than about people and their lifestyles. One of the practical implications of scientists' impatience with everyday life is the swing away from community-based, small-scale programs to supply-side strategies in the belief that it is easier to change nutrient intake by changing the environment of choices than it is to struggle with people's ability and willingness to change. Experience in developing countries provides ample evidence that this is a mistake. Many problems have been created in program planning through misunderstanding of important local beliefs and practices. A whole new genre of research strategies has grown up in the past decade aimed at ensuring that programs are planned and implemented in ways which recognise the importance of local environments. Chief among these strategies are Rapid Assessment Procedures (Scrimshaw & Gleason 1992; Scrimshaw & Hurtado 1987) and the increasing interest in Nutritional Anthropology (Pelto *et al.* 1989).

Most discussions of the success of Good Nutrition programs point to middle-class people as having 'better' eating (and other) habits in terms of the dietary guidelines. Middle-class people have a reputation for taking up healthy behaviours. The converse is often said of people with less education, lower occupational status, or less income.

With this in mind, some English researchers set out over a period of eighteen months to try to understand more about this greater awareness of health in a group of 28 middle-class families, each with two children aged between three and ten. They considered the families participating in the study to be well placed materially and socially to lead healthy lives. The researchers interviewed family members to examine their perceptions of health, illness and health-related behaviours in the social context of everyday domestic life (Backett 1990).

The participating parents could say what contributed to good health but found it difficult to put this into practice. They were also fairly sceptical about the efficacy of many health practices, even the ones they engaged in. One such sceptic was a scientist himself. In terms of scientific knowledge related to health, respondents perceived this as changing and unstable, and they reacted negatively to the moral tone of 'scientifically based health knowledge'. Similarly, people interviewed within the catchment area for the Heartbeat Wales project had their own theories about behaviour and health which were not taken into account by program planners. This 'lay epidemiology' could be a form of protection against the more exploitative aspects of health promotion messages.

Backett believes that the long duration of her study was crucial to the kind of information she collected. Most nutrition studies deal with people as individuals rather than as members of a household, take a 'one-off' sample of their food consumption, and rarely collect qualitative data such as interview material. Backett's study showed that people reported fewer health-promoting behaviours as time went on, partly due to a reduced need to maintain face for the interviewer.

In relation to nutrition, Backett reports a similar effect. What people first recorded as their diet changed in later interviews, partly for the kinds of practical reasons that come to light when people talk in detail about what they eat, but partly also because they felt less pressured to maintain a front. As time went on, 'they discussed more openly the pleasure and convenience aspects of so called "unhealthy" foods, and their everyday compromises to accommodate the taste of family members, particularly those of the children' (Backett 1990:63).

The children in the study were able to classify food as 'keeping you healthy' or 'not healthy', but they seemed to be more aware of the negative effects of unhealthy foods than the positive effects of healthy ones (Backett 1990:62). Most Good Nutrition program planners perceive everyday life as a problem per se and design strategies to overcome its exigencies, referring to 'barriers' to behaviour change. This underlies an almost universal assumption of Good Nutrition, that behaviour change is the only, or at least the most, worthwhile end-point of intervention programs. It is tempting to see, in this idea that what people currently do is unsatisfactory and should be changed, the seeds of all reform movements.

Just as Atwater and his colleagues 'knew' how their expert information and ideas should shape other people's behaviour, so too do the designers of many contemporary Good Nutrition programs. Everyday life marches to a different drummer from that represented in the nutrition expert's agenda. In this sense Good Nutrition is religious, persuading people to take up an ideal way of life, a form of 'right living', which few people, perhaps including the experts themselves, will successfully or willingly adopt in its totality.

A recent study based on a questionnaire concluded that one in two Australian adults were following dietary guidelines and branded the rest of the population as continuing to 'eat unhealthily' (CSIRO 1993:7). This conclusion is an unavoidable consequence of a community-wide reform model of Good Nutrition.

Part of the problem is the scientific dietary reformers' innate impatience with the social and behavioural sciences. Yet these sciences could do much to mitigate the chauvinistic aspects of the 'hard sciences' and encourage a more realistic appreciation of every-day life.

When individuals do profess belief in and take up recom-mended food habits, they do so very much on their own terms. Through everyday life, the experts' agenda is transformed into an amalgam which people find more compatible with their own needs and idiosyncrasies.

Some of the most interesting work exploring the difference between reported and actual food behaviour was conducted by anthropologists with two Italian-American communities. Using three different information gathering methods they were able to create a complete picture of how more than 200 households established their eating patterns and maintained and changed traditional practices (Goode *et al.* 1984). The researchers asked people to record what they ate over three days and also conducted extensive interviews. In addition, one of the researchers lived with four different families for a month each. The results of the study showed that the accounts people gave in interviews and records, especially with regard to ethnic customs, were idealised and influenced to some extent by childhood memories. Their closer observations of the families' every-day life revealed that when the idealised pattern collides with the realities of everyday life, compromise, or 'menu negotiation', occurs.

The families in the study belonged to a close-knit social network and there was a discernible pattern of meals which made up the 'ideal'. This ideal was based on a selected number of traditional meal types, which the researchers classified as 'gravy' (e.g. pasta with sauce), platter (meat or fish with separately served vegetables) and 'one-pot' (e.g. stews). This pattern was adapted according to the calendar (e.g. fish on Fridays), family commitments and recre-ational activities, occupational demands, who was present at the meal, and whose preferences had precedence.

Goode and her colleagues believe that nutrition research's cur-rent focus on foods and nutrients results from emphasising health as a justification for such investigations. However, if it is also important to understand why people eat as they do, other, everyday concepts must be included in researchers' frameworks, such as menus, meal planning, recipe repertoires and menu construction. These tap more complex systems than individual food choices. An appreciation of these concepts would enhance and humanise Good Nutrition programs, and make it clearer why some new practices are more acceptable than others and which ones are unlikely to be adopted at all.

Goode's findings underscored the importance of women's social networks in the maintenance of traditions and in mediating the adoption of new ideas and practices. Links between mothers and their daughters were particularly important when the daughters married and had their own families. Women talking with each other was another important influence on food practices, both the maintenance of the old and the adoption of the new. The way in which the women both praised and criticised each other, shared food, and developed and met their social obligations, constituted a kind of social control. In this case, however, the women themselves actively participated in making and maintaining the control.

The extent to which male preferences intrude on this process is unclear. As both Goode *et al.* and Counihan note, privileging male preferences is an important part of family life. At least in this case, the control is internal to the community and is a source of support and praise for women as well as criticism. It recognises skills and the women themselves are party to the 'web spinning' process, to use Scholte's term (quoted in Caplan 1988).

Children too can develop their own meanings for food. James' description of lolly-eating among a group of Northern English children illustrates some fascinating aspects of the 'extra-nutritional' value of food consumption. James first became aware of the children's practices when she realised that 'ket', a dialect word used to describe particular kinds of sweets, had roughly the same meaning as 'rubbish', that is, worthless. This was the word that adults applied to 'children's sweets': those with garish colours, sickly flavours, and non-food names and shapes like car parks, milk bottles and telephones. The manner in which these sweets were eaten and handled also emphasised their unadult nature. They were bought loose, kept in pockets and paper bags, offered around to friends for licks and sucks, and pulled in and out of mouths, especially to observe colour changes. James interprets her observations as demonstrating how the children made their own world separate from that of adults by inverting adult values. The fact that adults saw these sweets as rubbish made them all the more attractive (James 1979).

FOOD IDIOSYNCRASIES

We all have personal preferences, not only for particular foods but also for ways of serving and eating them. Some of our preferences,

The 12345+ Food & Nutrition Plan: the Australian version of 'Eating Right'

Indulgences or extras — No more than 2 serves

Meat and alternatives — 1 serve

Milk and milk products — 2 serves

Fruits — 3 serves

Vegetables — 4 serves

Breads, Cereals — 5+ serves

Source: CSIRO Division of Human Nutrition and the Anti-Cancer Foundation of South Australia

while important to us, may be so subtle they do not become obvious to us until we are unable to meet them.

Interviews with physically disabled people who rely on others to feed them have demonstrated just how minute and detailed such preferences can be and just how important they are. Something as mundane as bread and butter was variously preferred cut into small pieces, presented butter side down, or buttered right up to the edges (Crotty 1988). People also differ on the preferred sequence of foods—dry foods first, wet last; a bit of everything on the fork at once versus eating foods in sequence; large mouthfuls versus small; taking the cherry off the top first or leaving it until last; waiting for ice-cream to melt a bit first so that the sauce will make interesting swirls. The examples, and the variations, are endless. Some preferences are considered very important, others less so. Some may be reserved for special social occasions, others for when no one else is looking.

It is unclear how such a fundamentally human source of pleasure, creativity and individuality as the way we like to eat enters into Good Nutrition programs, yet such preferences and the beliefs which go with them may determine whether new food choices are adopted or existing practices dropped. Is there anywhere in the scientific literature a discussion, let alone a study, of the effect that pleasure in eating has on health?

Widdowson's paper on postwar German orphanages has shown how distress at mealtimes can be damaging to the growth of young, marginally nourished children. Unfortunately, next to nothing is known about the positive importance of pleasure in eating. It may be impossible for such a question to be asked within the cultural framework of scientific nutrition, which, in its reformist phase, springs from the same soil as the essentially moral association of pleasure in eating with fear of overconsumption and loss of control.

This issue may well lie at the heart of the conflict between scientific nutrition and everyday life. Because scientific nutrition may never be able to shed its moral and reformist heritage, it may always be saddled with a mission, that of justifying in scientific terms the process of social control, of 'putting the brakes on' the population at large. Perhaps this is the hidden cultural agenda for the scientific 'mass population approach' to Good Nutrition.

In making sense of our everyday lives, we are not passive victims. We 'seek to strategise within the constraints imposed' upon us (Caplan 1988:12): children by inverting adult rules; the disabled by 'domesticating' institutional mealtimes; Italian-American women by meeting men's preferences in main courses but serving as side dishes the foods they like themselves; and young middle-class families by adopting new behaviours only if they fit into their everyday life and by not expecting too much in the way of results.

Such everyday subversions are to be applauded because they represent, on a small scale, a resistance to the tyranny of expertise—expertise which, largely because of an unquestioning acceptance of its own beneficence, fails to consult or fully inform those whom it seeks to change.

Just as it is important for dietary reformers to understand what ordinary people do and the strategies they use to cope with everyday life, it is equally important that lay people have access to information, discussion and debate about what experts do and what strategies they employ to manage their everyday environments.

91

Experts, whether they be individuals, government agencies, food companies, health practitioners or heart and cancer associations, can create anxiety in the lay public as they use their technical knowledge, privileged position, resources and access to the media to exert pressure on the community. It seems fair that the lay public should have the power to hurt the experts' markets, profits, funds or reputations if they abuse their position or breach community trust. There should be an open critique of Good Nutrition programs and of the use of implied health threats in the marketing of products such as high-fibre breakfast cereals and high-calcium milks.

LAY RESISTANCE TO DIETARY REFORM

Lay people sometimes object to being told what to eat in a moralising and threatening way. This perspective may be overlooked in policy and program planning but it is alive and well in humour. Examples can be found in cartoons and in short newspaper and magazine articles. The 'Anxiety page', by the humorist Patrick Cook is a classic of the genre. The themes he introduces include the connection of healthy eating with a denial of sensuality, decreased pleasure in eating and less enjoyment in life (Cook, 1991). In the words of a dieting workshop participant: 'Eating for health is like sex for procreation'.

Ordinary people can have an uninvited impact on policy and programs. Discussing health and welfare programs in Mexico, Sherraden notes the 'weapons' that powerless groups can turn on official policy: foot dragging, dissimulation, desertion, false compliance, pilfering, feigned ignorance, slander, arson, and sabotage. Communities, then, are quite capable not only of not participating in programs but also of actively resisting them and, in extreme circumstances, dismantling them (Sherraden 1991).

THE EVERYDAY LIFE OF EXPERTS: STUDYING UP

Laura Nader (1988) has written about how anthropology might be reinvented so as to provide useful information to citizens about the workings of their society, especially those institutions that govern and shape policy. Traditionally, anthropologists study exotic cultures and people different from themselves. Not only that, they usually 'study down', especially outside their own culture. According to

Nader, fieldwork conducted by anthropologists in the United States is much more likely to focus on the poor, ethnic minorities and the disadvantaged than on the middle and upper classes. Theories developed from studies of such skewed populations may thus be biased.

Nader is concerned with how anthropology might ask questions from the point of view of the less powerful in society. The equivalent of this in nutrition research would be asking questions that give due weight to the problems of everyday life: How does Good Nutrition as a top-down process impinge on families and individuals? Do weight-control programs make life better for women? Do dietitians find it easier than others to control their weight, or are they doubly disadvantaged because they have to promote weight control as well as be thin? Do Good Nutrition programs meet their agenda of scientifically reforming of diet at the expense of the everyday needs of the community?

Instead of 'studying up', perhaps there should be a renewed emphasis on 'asking up'. Good Nutrition could drop its reformist stance and give the general public more information about how food production works, what policy and personal behaviour options exist, and how policy decisions are made. Good Nutrition could represent the community's everyday interests rather than merely reform its behaviour.

8

A theoretical framework

 Is there any question that the currencies of exchange of primary importance in culture are these three: food, sex, talk. Through the interaction of these three, we endow relationships with value and invest them with meaning through intercourse of several sorts. (Abrahams 1984:19–36)

We should be on our guard not to overestimate science and scientific methods when it is a question of human problems; and we should not assume that experts are the only ones who have a right to express themselves on questions affecting the organisation of society. (Albert Einstein, quoted in Waring 1988)

NUTRITION EDUCATION IS A CULTURAL ACTIVITY

Good Nutrition is a cultural activity in the sense that it is not conducted on the basis of some objective 'truth'. It is not determined by a set of factual certainties or unarguable values which allow us to think of it as 'right'. Rather it is an agreed-upon activity, created by people, not by 'scientific facts'. Even when a campaign is conducted with reference to particular 'facts', it can never take all known facts into account. People select the facts to be used and decide how they will be applied in social action.

We are prepared to believe that individuals have different ways of viewing health. This is the basis of the Health Belief Model, one of a number of models used by health educators to predict and explain health behaviour. This model suggests that much of people's health behaviour depends on: What things they are concerned about, how concerned they are about them, whether they think there is something they can do about these things, how well they think they might be able to do this, and how effective they think that action might be.

A similar schema could be said to apply at the societal level as is illustrated by the nature and content of nutrition education in the US in the mid-1940s. Practical reasons made food conservation and health high priorities. This was translated into admonishments to the populace to be patriotic by behaving in ways prescribed by experts. The preoccupation in the 1970s and 1980s with the 'epidemic of killer diseases', principally coronary heart disease is another instance. Today, however, there is more scope for discussing and redefining which problems should be addressed. It would have been very difficult in the 1940s to raise a debate about whether the war was the 'real' issue for Good Nutrition.

Today decision makers agree that chronic disease prevention by diet will be the priority in nutrition programs and policies, and determine that the social action flowing from this will rest on strategies of dietary reform. How might things be different?

What is society concerned about?

Nutrition education and policy focus on the category (heart disease) in which most deaths occur, because this is viewed as a 'diet-related disease' whose incidence can be effectively reduced by changing eating behaviour. This conclusion is a policy decision, not an immutable scientific truth. Other decision-makers with other motivations could conceivably choose differently, in which case other decisions might now be guiding nutrition policy.

What is a serious problem?

There are various ways in which this could be assessed. It might be the problem that causes the most deaths or the most suffering, that affects the most people, or the group to whom we owe most (children, for example) or perhaps the one that costs society the most in financial terms.

What is a feasible and effective strategy?

It is possible to view some problems as very serious but unlikely to be effectively overcome because no satisfactory strategy is available.

At all these stages, judgments are involved. The people most likely to participate in making these judgments, so far as nutrition is concerned, are what Veatch calls 'knowledge experts', plus government bureaucrats and politicians (Veatch 1991). The relationship between the solutions proposed and the way problems are defined can be seen in the history of social action programs addressing malnutrition in developing countries. In the 1940s and 1950s the emphasis was on freedom from hunger, but malnutrition was treated principally as a medical issue. The oil crisis of the 1970s coincided with an emphasis on the overall food supply and on access to sufficient food for the poor. There was more direct action in this period, including food-price stabilisation, social security efforts, and the development of special health care services for women and children. More recently, the World Bank and the United Nations Development Program have emphasised the importance of economic growth (and of engaging the poor in this process), social security measures, and the development of human resources, which are seen as essential both to economic growth and to the success of social security efforts. In each 'phase' the same end-point, malnutrition has been addressed, but different views of the problem have led to different answers. It is to be hoped that each view would develop appropriate and effective answers to the problem but, as Field has pointed out, this has not always been so (Field 1985, 1987). Programs driven by what he refers to as 'machine theory', or the 'plan and control' approach, may fail at the implementation stage, principally because these models are weak at taking into account practical issues of management and everyday life. This may render them vulnerable to a fatal inflexibility.

NUTRITION EXPERTS AS POLICYMAKERS

Accepting experts in scientific nutrition (the knowledge experts) as equally expert policymakers and advocates of social action should be tempered with some caution. Knowledge experts are not necessarily expert in making evaluative judgments about the use of their knowledge or about the ethical questions its application implies. Program planners using biological knowledge as a basis for social action are predisposed toward 'plan and control' strategies. Moreover, the literature and scientific discourse which support the 'lipocentric' view of nutrition policy and nutrition education are biased.

Veatch (1991) makes a distinction between possessing knowledge in an area and making decisions about the use of that knowledge. He maintains that clinicians' decisions about prescribing a particular treatment are logically independent of the related scientific knowledge they possess. The way in which experts use their knowledge involves judgments, and the values they employ in making those judgments cannot necessarily be seen as more 'correct' or more appropriate than those employed by non-experts. Veatch offers the example of the change in treatment of cancer from heroic measures to prolong the life of terminally ill patients to a more careful consideration of the patient's quality of life. This change did not depend on clinicians' expertise but on pressure from lay sections of the community whose values were different from those of knowledge experts on this issue.

The values that experts employ in making their judgments may vary among individual experts and among different groups of experts. For example, psychologists' assessment of ethical conflicts in research has been shown to vary between men and women, recent graduates and those who have had their degrees longer, and perhaps more importantly here, between researchers and practitioners. Ethical issues were seen as less important by psychologists who were male, who were researchers rather than practitioners, trained in areas of basic rather than applied psychology, and had held their highest degree for some time (Kimmel 1991). Kimmel has noted that scientists tend to overrate the importance of their work and to underestimate potential harms as studies get closer to commencement. Both factors could lead to reduced perceptions of the importance of ethical issues. This is particularly relevant to the US National Institutes of Health's consensus conference on high blood cholesterol levels and what the approach to this problem should be. In developing a consensus on such a controversial issue, value judgments need to be made about the risks and benefits of various approaches and their costs relative to other priorities, decisions which, as Veatch notes, cannot be made on the basis of science alone.

Over the past decade, the National Institutes of Health has sponsored a number of consensus conferences, at which an issue such as obesity is discussed by a selected group of experts and after which a statement representing a consensus of their views is released. Skrabanek, one of the harshest critics of this method, believes it is undemocratic and ineffective. He says participating experts are carefully selected for their views and that only token dissidents are included. He notes that the consensus statement

97

which was the basis for the US National Cholesterol Education Program endorsed a diet whose effectiveness in reducing coronary heart disease risk had not been demonstrated, indeed Skrabanek asserts that there was not a 'scrap of evidence' to support it (Skrabanek 1990).

The effect of values on 'scientific' recommendations is illustrated by a recent Australian statement on the management of hyperlipidaemia. A 1991 consensus conference jointly sponsored by the Pharmaceutical Benefits Advisory Committee, the National Heart Foundation and the National Health and Medical Research Council developed a statement to ' . . . guide clinicians in the appropriate management of individual hyperlipidaemic patients . . . and to help the government develop pharmaceutical benefit policies'. In its introduction, the statement concedes that it is not clear to what extent existing treatments apply to women and older people. The statement deserves credit for this, and for its recognition that heart disease prevention programs have had no impact on total mortality. However, the issue of whether women benefit from current treatments (even though they pose some risk to them) has had no effect at all on the recommendations. No reservations are expressed about the adoption of low-fat diets, apart from noting possible problems when women do adopt them. In the final section on 'Future directions', it is recommended that high priority be given to further research on the impact of lipid lowering in the elderly. The statement says nothing about the need for further research on the effectiveness or otherwise of treatments for women.

In his book *Heart Failure* (1989), the American journalist Thomas Moore investigates why and how heart disease has become so central to the politics of medicine and medical research in the US. He devotes a number of chapters to the recent history of the diet–heart hypothesis and the preventive approach taken in the US. The chapter on a consensus meeting held on this topic reveals the disagreement among experts and the politics behind the final report. Among a number of criticisms of the conference report, Moore cites its failure to reflect a balance of the evidence presented; the avoidance of central issues, in particular the evidence that prevention programs have not lowered total mortality, and the suppression of legitimate dissent in the discussions, including the refusal of a request for a minority report on the grounds that it was inconsistent with a consensus. Moore quotes one of the experts attending the conference as saying: 'We all have the same set of prepackaged data that we thaw over the fire of our own prejudices' (Moore 1989:61).

None of this implies that scientists wilfully set out to mislead anyone. Making decisions about social action inevitably involves evaluative judgments. The best scientists as well as the worst will always be a part of this process. This in itself does not constitute a problem, *unless* policy-making is not recognised as a value-based process. At best, orthodoxies develop, dissenting views are ignored or suppressed and new, possibly more appropriate ideas are not generated. At worst, current programs which cause problems are continued for longer than they might otherwise have been.

Veatch and Moreno (1991) point to the basic flaw in basing social action on such consensus statements by making the distinction between the development of a consensus and the correctness of that consensus.

A good example of the selective use and omission of 'difficult' data favouring the retention of the status quo is given by Nestle in a discussion of the preparation of the US Surgeon General's Report on Nutrition and Health—a widely quoted authority justifying dietary guideline–based nutrition programs. Nestle says the draft report justified creating a national priority for dietary reform on the basis of Americans' overconsumption of fat. During the preparation of the final report, however, successive experts reviewed the evidence on fat consumption in the US, and subsequently the report's editorial committee could not arrive at a consensual interpretation of the data. Because of methodological flaws in the research underlying the chapter, the editors refused to interpret what the data indicated about Americans' fat consumption over time (Nestle 1990:141).

Rather than publicise this debate and the scientists' uncertainties, the chapter was dropped from the report. The report, however, is widely used, including in Australia, as a reference point in arguing for dietary reform. In an article reviewing recent controversial statements about the efficacy of lowering cholesterol levels, Glanz argues that it is important for health educators to know about criticisms of the diet–heart theory and be able to respond to them (Glanz 1990:89). But in setting out to help health promotion practitioners make sense of this complex controversy, Glanz is ultimately reduced to appealing to particular reports:

> For those who question the effectiveness of diet for reducing blood cholesterol, the support for dietary means of risk reduction has been affirmed more strongly than ever before in the last three years. Major documents, which supersede earlier authoritative reports and underscore the role of nutrition in chronic disease control, were released

in 1988 by the Surgeon General's Office and in 1989 by the National Research Council of the National Academy of Sciences. (Glanz 1990:93)

The decision not to publish certain material may be just as important to public discussion and debate as what is published. The case of the Surgeon General's report may be an example of negative or ambiguous findings being swept under the carpet, a phenomenon which has been shown to apply to the type of articles published in both technical journals and in newspapers (Koren & Klein 1991; Easterbrook *et al.* 1990). There is a bias against what could be construed as 'bad news' for those who hold the prevailing theory. Yet it is the inclusion of the 'bad news' alongside the 'good news' that is essential for rational debate. Glanz's article attempted a degree of honesty unusual in this field, yet her effort was undermined by the biased construction of the Surgeon General's report. What would Glanz have concluded about dietary reform if the chapter referred to by Nestle had been published?

ARE THE VALUES OF KNOWLEDGE EXPERTS SHARED BY THE WIDER COMMUNITY?

The growth and development of nutrition knowledge offers gains to scientists and to 'science'. Careers are based, and made, on scientists' commitment to hypotheses such as the diet–heart theory. The same careers may be further advanced as the theories change. A knowledge expert's career and professional satisfaction may advance through developing and promoting and then changing a theory. This can be seen as the positive growth of knowledge and understanding in nutrition. But as theories are selected for application in social action and then revised, non-participants, those who are on the receiving end or, in Black's terms, the 'sharp end' of community programs, can be seen as unequal and in many cases reluctant respondents.

There seems to be the basis of an ethical dilemma here. The 'normal' process of knowledge growth and application builds careers for the knowledge creators and those who implement programs, but the population is made to eddy and swirl in response. Selective social action without equal participation by the community becomes limited, in Aronson's terms, to an entrepreneurial strategy of nutrition science. Funding and kudos follow areas of research which have an obvious social application in human health and welfare, but the benefit to the community may not match the benefits to nutrition science and nutrition experts. In addition, health workers get caught in this gap, and are forced to choose whose interests they represent. In the case of nutrition, will it be the nutrition experts' reform agenda or the more diverse concerns of the community groups from whose needs and interests they earn a living?

In addition, corporate interests use selected aspects of the reform agenda for commercial gain, but the health and information gains of this practice for the community are uncertain.

Obviously, people do not take in reformers' advice like sponges, but the knowledge makers and appliers' understanding of their 'mission' does not readily accommodate the notion of resistance. Feedback does not prompt them to change direction, but only to use the information to 'increase the effectiveness' of the same actions.

This creates social relationships which advantage the tinkerers but in the process entirely omit the views and values of the wider community and of those inclined to embed their conclusions in the reality of everyday life. Nor do organised consumer representatives necessarily redress the inequity, for they too may be committed to diet–heart dietary reform, seeing themselves as part of the expert value system. Yet consumer groups could engage this system in a debate as equals (as distinct from being non-experts accepting expert opinion) if they developed questions based on values and ethical dilemmas rooted in community interests. Is it right that the debate about dietary reform is not held in view of the public? Is it right that people, particularly women, are persuaded to adopt a particular set of food choices without being told the likely benefits and limitations of such choices? Why aren't women's health concerns on the consumerist agenda in this regard? The reform of nutrition experts is yet to gain a foothold in consumer activism.

IMPLEMENTATION OF SOCIAL ACTION

There is plenty of experience of nutrition policy development and implementation to draw on for a sense of direction. There is much evidence that large-scale, comprehensive and complex planning is an albatross, yet this is precisely the direction that nutrition policy is taking in developed countries. This approach is probably derived from the realisation of the many factors which influence food consumption. This is clearly shown when the Australian 'food and nutrition' system is identified (Heywood & Lund-Adams 1991; Worsley 1991), however, as Field notes, this does not necessarily imply that the implementation of policies should rely on similarly complex strategies. On the contrary, experience in developing countries suggests that when participation by the wider community, such as changes in behaviour is the aim, the most successful programs are those which are flexible in local application and sympathetic to local participation.

Field, a policy analyst who has worked in developing countries, points out that nutrition expertise alone has never been sufficient to conduct successful dietary reform programs and has on occasions introduced problems. Multisectoral Nutrition Planning, which was declared a failure not long after it became the dominant model for tackling malnutrition, would have been recognised as having a low likelihood of success, says Field, if the available, 'unheeded literature', on policy implementation had been read by the advocates of the method (Field 1985).

Some strategies advocated by diet–heart nutrition policy advocates bear close similarities to those which have been shown to be less than successful in the context of developing countries. Such experience suggests that nutrition policy-makers should give higher priority to implementation issues and avoid the inappropriate application of expert knowledge.

Technical experts often see implementation as a logical extension of the policy-making process itself rather than as the often conflictual and intrinsically messy process of managing the practicalities of a 'real life' program. Field variously refers to this technical view as mechanical theory, the following of 'blueprints', and the neglect of the 'black box' between planning and evaluation (Field 1985). Field has described a program of community involvement in nutrition and general health in India which has been effective precisely because it permitted conflict and 'messiness'. Although central planning is attractive to experts, he says, the control and orderliness it seems to promise are usually illusory, especially when a program must be implemented locally. Creative adaptations in the process of implementation are important for success.

COMMUNITY REPRESENTATION IN THE DEVELOPMENT OF NUTRITION POLICY

The nutrition policy analyst Nancy Milio has published (1990) what is probably the first wide-ranging discussion of how nutrition policy is made. She focuses on Norway, which developed a national policy in the 1970s, but she also refers to other countries, particularly the United States. Milio's book demonstrates that the main focus of nutrition policy in the West is not so much diet as one component of that diet: fat. She states: 'The most problematic goal-setting issue in nutrition policymaking is the degree and quality of dietary fat reduction' (Milio 1990:15).

It seems that in diet–heart policies, diets rather than people are the primary concern. Milio certainly seems to take this view, which is based on technical rationality. In the case of dietary fat reduction, scientific and technical knowledge are used to justify particular courses of social action without reference to the implications for the effects of this action on, or their interplay with, people's everyday life. Dietary reform is seen as a technical issue which only requires the application of scientific knowledge to fix the problem. It is perhaps an unhappy portent that Milio does not refer to Field's work at all.

Although this book received favourable comment in scientific journals, at least two reviewers noted the excessively 'top-down, centralist' nature of its policymaking model and its lack of discussion about how to ensure representation of the wider community at decision-making levels (e.g. Edema 1991). In a specifically Australian example, Chapman follows a similar path to Milio and in doing so illuminates some additional problems that this approach creates (Chapman 1990).

Chapman's chief concern is the improvement of community nutrition and he discusses the most appropriate roles for a variety of agencies—government, non-government and private-sector. Chapman sees the role of health workers and government bureaucrats in advancing nutrition policy as limited and concludes that the main players in terms of influencing what Australians eat are industry, non-government professional associations and agencies, and government departments of health, agriculture, primary industry and consumer affairs. Asserting that the Australian diet is 'aberrant' and that intersectoral action is the most desirable way to achieve dietary reform through 'the development of consumer demand in the right direction', he dismisses local-level action to improve nutrition as 'parochial little interventions and events', and government health education efforts as well-intentioned but small in scale and with little effect. Large-scale interventions, then, may be born out of impatience with the alternative, a picture quite at odds with the 'unheeded literature' referred to by Field.

Chapman and Milio share an uncritical acceptance of 'top-down' dietary reform. This view completely disdains community participation and is uninterested in the everyday life of the people who are the supposed beneficiaries of policies. When diet, not people, is the focus, the technical rationalist position becomes far easier to adopt. In a very real sense Glanz, Milio and Chapman are only partially engaged in the debate because their acceptance of its technical rationality precludes them from interrogating the appropriateness of the policies they discuss. Because their analysis is only partial, they are not in a position to adopt Berger's ethic of responsibility, which presupposes acceptance of the consequences of one's actions. This, for a technical-rationalist nutrition expert, would entail acquiring detailed information about the likely consequences of nutrition programs. Very few nutrition experts have such information. If they joined the debate from a social perspective, however, they would be able to question the appropriateness of diet–heart nutrition policies in the context of everyday realities. From this point of view, local-level efforts might no longer seem like 'parochial little interventions'—and parochial little interventions might begin to look more humane.

REPRESENTING THE COMMUNITY

The case has been made for the need to include community-wide views in the process of creating Good Nutrition and nutrition policy, and for creating implementation strategies which are locally appropriate and recognise community participation as a factor in success. This is based largely on the argument that decisions about what social action should follow from nutrition knowledge are based on value judgments and that wider community values should have at least equal consideration with those of nutrition knowledge experts. The fact that 'the community' will be expected to act on and implement much that flows from such endeavours further reinforces the importance of taking the realities of everyday life into account in the making and especially the implementation of policy.

It is time for Good Nutrition to strike a new balance wherein the uncertainty of gains and the potential for problems are both given weight. There are a number of ways in which this could be done.

THE VALUES FRAMEWORK OF NUTRITION POLICY

An explicit framework of values for a nutrition policy would recognise at least two important things: first, that policies are indeed based on values, not just technical knowledge, and second, that the values which underpin such a policy can be made explicit. My argument has also supported the idea that priority in implementation strategies should be given to practical knowledge and the contingencies and values of everyday life because however out of place the privileging of expert knowledge may be at the policy-making level, it is many times more so in implementation strategies. A nutrition policy could be developed specifically stating that the household was the social unit around which priorities and strategies would be focused. Strategies could be evaluated through household-impact assessments. 'Supply side' strategies would not be precluded in such a policy, but the basis for evaluating them would be a social unit rather than a technical concept (the national average diet). The values underpinning such a policy would be radically different from those currently in play in affluent countries. They would include, for example, asking what extra costs are incurred by households in responding to nutrition campaigns; what are the consequences to the household of changed food preparation techniques: what adaptations are families with two employed parents making in preparing and serving meals?

AUSTRALIAN NATIONAL FOOD AND NUTRITION POLICY

The hegemony of medical thinking and the dearth of social and especially critical perspectives in the research basis for nutrition policy are clearly illustrated in the draft food and nutrition policy developed for the federal department of Health, Housing and Community Services. Epidemiology is identified as the preferred research framework for nutrition researchers. While the implications of this are not entirely clear (Should all nutrition-linked research be epidemiological research? Should all researchers think only in terms of populations?), the message is: epidemiological research is of most value to nutrition policy. The draft policy notes that the kind of research which should be encouraged is that which would help achieve the objectives of the policy.

If this becomes the dominant research ideology, where will the critical knowledge come from to identify problems and change

105

strategy in accord with experience? The 'plan and control' model of implementation based on what Field calls mechanical theory is currently central to nutrition policy. Epidemiological research will not pick up program errors, help overcome practical glitches or give implementers feedback on community views. Case studies of implementation in action might do this, action research with practitioners might, ethnographic studies with small groups of people might, understanding the experience of, for example, developing countries and nutrition planners in the 1970s might. Good research, which makes use of past experience in nutrition policy and planning, will certainly demonstrate that this type of food and nutrition policy is much more difficult to implement than is currently appreciated, particularly by medically and biologically trained knowledge experts.

The consequences of recognising the limitations of mechanical theory and the importance of community participation in nutrition policy and practice may be change, not in community dietary reform but in the nature of Good Nutrition itself.

CRITICAL THEORY AND GOOD NUTRITION

While it may be interesting to look at both historical and contemporary Good Nutrition for their own sakes, a wider framework within which to view this critique is needed. In particular, a theoretical framework enables deeper examination of individual issues and allows the possibility of connecting the present analysis to a wider discourse. Critical theory is used here because it is particularly sympathetic to theory–practice problems and it offers the possibility of addressing the disjunction between experts' views and the realities of everyday life. In fact it has set itself the task, among others, of welding theory and practice together. Critical theory is especially useful in analysing issues of authoritarian expertise and the inappropriate application of scientific knowledge to social action. It attempts to combine a philosophical with a scientific approach to understanding society through:

- appealing to a widened notion of rationality. (It is possible to reason solely by reference to scientific facts or, as has been argued here, to include ethical and social values in reasoning about a problem, for example, dietary reform)
- resisting all forms of domination and giving central importance to the idea of emancipation

- exploring the ways in which knowledge areas such as science are practised (van Manen 1990).

In critical theory, clear distinctions are made between three types of knowledge generation or science: that which searches for objective truth (biochemical aspects of nutrition would fit here); that which searches for meaning and understanding (such as ethnographic studies of the food procurement strategies of low-income families); and that which involves a critical perspective, or 'reflection in action'. In the latter case, individuals identify a problem, develop an understanding of the problem and decide upon appropriate action. The individuals could be dietitians or they could be people living in poverty. In both instances, 'reflection in action' refers to the individuals' own actions and not to others' actions. So, for example, dietitians who identify the low-fat eating programs they conduct as creating problems for families with few resources would reflect on what they themselves (not their clients) might change to alleviate the problem they have identified.

Critical theory focuses on communication as the link between the more and less powerful and is interested in distortions of communication and the possibility that they can be corrected. When applied to birthing practices, it has shown the gap in communication between doctors and their obstetrics clients. Scambler (1987) notes that as a result of a number of factors, many historical, birth became redefined as pathological, or at least potentially hazardous to health. Since whoever defines the problem controls the situation, it thus became the province of medical expertise. The shifting of childbirth into hospitals increased medical experts' control, and simultaneously decreased women's control, over the process of birth. Midwives and other non-medical birth attendants came under the supervision of doctors, who also retained control of drugs, machines and procedures associated with childbirth and were in a position to control the distribution and direction of research funds and the nature of government policies on childbirth. Defining pregnant women as 'at risk' legitimated and promoted hospitalisation and the medical control of childbirth.

Since the rise of the women's movement, a number of concessions have been won for women having babies, including more humane 'birthing centres', most within hospitals; the possibility of 'home birth'; and more respect for the women's wishes with regard to the place and manner of giving birth.

Whatever the benefits of better medical care for women, the extent of medical control over birthing practices cannot be explained or justified solely in technical terms. Critical theory sees childbirth as an example of what it calls 'the medical colonisation of the lifeworld'. Nutrition policy is another example. The definition of entire populations as 'at risk' (or, in Rose's term, 'sick') and Senator George McGovern's florid description of healthy people as malnourished illustrate how eating behaviour has been transformed into the legitimate concern of doctors. Doctors and those who share their vision are therefore given the longest and most respectful hearing on what nutrition policy's aims should be (the treatment and prevention of chronic disease), which kind of nutrition research should be prioritised and funded (epidemiological), what food people should eat and what the 'entire food and nutrition system' should focus on. The medical perspective on nutrition is a legitimate and important one, but there are other, as yet relatively powerless, views.

Carr and Kemmis extrapolate from critical theory to a 'critical social science', and it is the latter which will probably be the more useful in reinventing Good Nutrition. A critical social science is drawn from the problems of everyday life and can address itself to solving them. It is critical in the sense not only of pointing out problems but also of looking at the historical development of aspects of everyday life which systematically disadvantage some people while advantaging others. It pays particular attention to the forms of disadvantage (e.g. women's in childbirth) which impose meanings on people's lives which are not consonant with their own experiences or their aspirations. It is concerned with 'ways of thinking which support such subjugation whether in the oppression of one class by another, or in the dominance of a way of thinking which makes such oppression seem unproblematic, inevitable, incidental, or even justified' (Carr & Kemmis:138).

Although Carr and Kemmis's work is directed mainly towards teachers and the everyday issues they deal with, the principles they set out are relevant to health care practitioners. In particular they will be used here to indicate some possibilities for health workers, especially dietitians, who are at the 'sharp end' of Good Nutrition.

The Patrick Cook cartoon mentioned earlier expresses a popular view of the dietitian: female, thin-lipped, slim, punitive and a killjoy. Dietitians cope with this view in part by becoming professionalised and by being recognised for the application of their medical-scientific knowledge. They attend annual conferences which discuss 'power', 'communication' and professional status. In a very real sense they can become victims, as well as perpetrators, of the distorted communication which arises from an excessively medicalised view of eating. As women (in Australia, 95 per cent of dietitians are women) they are influenced by social messages about being responsible for family health, and the need to be slim and act on Good Nutrition messages. But they are doubly affected in the sense that their professional identity is tied up in persuading other people, also mostly women, to do this. When dietitians' clients are men, they seek to influence their female partners, because they are almost invariably responsible for food preparation.

A British study has demonstrated that when a man has diabetes, his wife changes her food choices to conform with his diet. When a woman becomes diabetic, however, her husband's diet does not change in a direction which could be construed as being supportive of her (Probert, Maddison & Roland 1990).

Given the practical, down-to-earth nature of the communications dietitians have with clients, reflection on this kind of process could humanise the dietary reform movement. However, dietitians do not (at least publicly) value this aspect of their practice, preferring to see diet as a technology in which they have particular knowledge and skills. There is little discussion of how dietitians do their work, or of how their work is received by their clients. The privileging of science as a way of understanding their work leads to an emphasis on objective, measurable cause-and-effect relationships. If technique A leads to more weight loss in women than technique B, for example, it is automatically judged to be 'better'.

Quantitative, medical-scientific research is important, but why is it the dominant form? What other forms of research might inform dietetic practice? To enhance the professional satisfaction of dietitians and improve their usefulness to their clientele, we may need to go outside the medical model and address the way dietitians talk to clients, how dietitians organise their work, and what dissatisfactions they experience in their practice. In reality, dietitians may often make complex trade-offs in helping patients adjust to altered food choices. The health educator Digby Anderson (1979) counsels caution in adapting research from other knowledge areas to dietetic practice. For example, educational or communication theory is sometimes said to be appropriate for dietitians, as their role could be seen as educational—teaching about diet. In transcribed interviews between English dietitians and their clients, however, Anderson discerns much more than information exchange. Dietitians listened without interruption to their clients' stories even when their purport seemed tangential to the business at hand. Such stories may give dietitians important clues about their clients' social context. Clients do not give well-ordered and organised statements of their eating behaviour, but provide the information 'wrapped up in stories'. It is this story-telling which 'commands the dietitian's tolerance' (Anderson:190). A more socially oriented study of dietitians (or other practitioners) giving individual advice may lead to a better understanding of community-wide nutrition programs.

The act of swallowing divides nutrition's two worlds: the post-swallowing sciences of biology, physiology, biochemistry and pathology and the pre-swallowing culture of behaviour, society and experience. Giving adequate emphasis to the pre-swallowing world could help nutrition practitioners develop a more humane and more effective approach to Good Nutrition.

A 'WIDENED NOTION OF RATIONALITY'

Clinical medicine has recognised for some time that a 'widened notion of rationality' is an important part of practice. When logical deductions from medical theories were the rational basis of medical practice (if problems are caused by 'lack of oxygen', then fresh air must be good for you), the result was often the introduction of ineffective and harmful treatments. Even when a medical theory is based on sound research, the mechanisms involved in disease are so complex that the theory may not necessarily be able to accurately predict whether a treatment will be harmful or effective.

Speculative theories became unacceptable as a basis for medical practice in the nineteenth century. Theories were subsequently based on the results of controlled experiments and clinical trials. More recently, the desirability or otherwise of treatment effects has become an essential consideration. Medical decision-making today grapples with ethics and values, the non-biological, cultural components of medical practice. The clinical practitioner must think humanistically and realise that good patient care includes consideration of quality-of-life and ethical issues.

GOOD PRACTICE IS MUCH MORE THAN BIOLOGY

Given that ethics and values have been thoroughly incorporated into clinical decision-making, a nutrition policy and practice which suppresses uncertainty and is chauvinistically medically oriented would seem a bit outdated. Good Nutrition must address the question of whose interests it is serving or, more importantly, not serving as a matter of urgency.

A debate that has raged for a decade in the developing world, over the philosophical underpinnings of primary health care (PHC), is particularly relevant to Good Nutrition. Many PHC programs in developing countries are concerned either directly or indirectly with nutrition, for example, food-supplementation programs for children under five. Child growth monitoring projects and agricultural development programs could also be said to be indirect nutrition programs.

Some have seen the debate as being between two irreconcilable approaches to the role of PHC in health development (Rifkin & Walt 1986). The first approach emphasises the efficacy of interventions and the need to transfer technologies that will improve health quickly, while the second is based on a conviction that technologies will only be effective if they are appropriately integrated into the societies that use them. In short, the stand-off is one of 'programs versus process'. The programs focus is allied philosophically to the expert-knowledge, 'plan and control' model of Good Nutrition.

The PHC debate erupted when the idea of 'selective primary health care' (SPHC) was raised. It was argued that a focus on specific problems, especially where resources were scarce, would lead to better health outcomes in a shorter time—in other words, get results in medical terms. SPHC attracts foreign support to targeted programs in developing countries because it produces recordable results, encourages private-sector involvement in health care delivery, is apparently cost-effective, promotes the use of advanced technologies (which benefits multinational corporations) and maintains the financial and institutional status quo. However, critics have pointed out that SPHC negates the concept of community participation, prioritises some diseases but neglects others, reinforces authoritarian attitudes, has a fragile scientific basis, and has questionable moral and ethical implications because it allows foreign and elitist interests to overrule those of the majority of people. In contradistinction, PHC is seen by its supporters not as an alternative form of health care delivery but a strategy for 'developing' health in communities. It emphasises process—the way in which programs are conducted—in particular the extent to which local communities participate in the planning, conduct and evaluation of health-related activities. The two approaches are distinguished by different ways of working with communities and different goals and expectations of programs.

111

The process approach distinguishes between PHC services and PHC per se. PHC prioritises process and change rather than promoting programs designed to be repeated and replicated. Rifkin and Walt believe that 'SPHC has confined "health" to a narrow meaning in the control of those trained to deal with disease' (1986:561).

The parallels with Scambler's comments on the medicalisation of childbirth and the current critique of Good Nutrition are obvious. In the struggle to make health care accessible and equitable, more powerful interests are better placed than 'ordinary' people to claim the debate and decide which models will dominate. Changing this situation will require the 'ordinary', the non- and the less-expert to claim their right to participate in spinning their own web.

The United Nations Declaration of Alma-Ata is the 'parent' of all 'Health for All' efforts. The Australian national nutrition policy claims to be part of this effort. In appealing to the declaration for its justification, it must seek the outcome of better health and better quality of life, not only better nutrition. The principal document for seeking better health outcomes in Australia has virtually ensured the complete subsumption of Good Nutrition under coronary heart disease and cancer prevention at the level of federal government policy (Department of Health, Housing and Community Services 1993). If nutrition policy and Good Nutrition seek outcomes only in terms of chronic disease, this privileges those with medical expertise and confines the solution to minor variations of a dietary technology (the dietary guidelines) through a 'plan and control' agenda for dietary reform.

Two examples of food and nutrition programs not dependent on a medical conceptualisation are the idea of household food security and caring capacity and the access of women to community life and politics through their experience of food.

The UN Subcommittee on Nutrition defines a household as food secure when 'it has access to the food needed for a healthy life for all its members (adequate in terms of quality, quantity, safety and culturally acceptable), and when it is not at undue risk of losing such access' (ACC/SCN 1991:5). Household food security has been recognised in the draft Australian nutrition policy, but in its medicalised form. Low-income households' lack of food security is seen as prejudicing their nutritional status. However, it is not necessary to appeal to what is ultimately a biological reason to justify a better deal for low-income families in this regard. The most painful aspects of being poor in an affluent society are the necessity to choose between equally important requirements and the constraints within which families must constantly live. By and large, the chief food problem for low-income families is not the lack of food (although this is true for some), but rather the cost to the family in decreased enjoyment and satisfaction and missed leisure opportunities after food, fuel and rent are paid for. Allowing people to pay fixed-cost bills in small instalments may be of great assistance in contributing to household food security in its broadest definition. Co-operation between nutritionists and government and other agencies to create accessible leisure activities and opportunities for shared meals in pleasant social settings could be comfortably accommodated within the UN definition and the PHC concern for 'developing' health through participation in local activities.

The UN Subcommittee on Nutrition defines caring capacity thus:

"Care" in general refers to the provision in the household and the community of time, attention and support to meet the physical, mental and social needs of the growing child and other family members. It leads to the optimal use of human, economic and organizational resources. At an extreme, lack of "care" is neglect. In the context of nutrition, most importantly it facilitates:

- optimal use of household food resources for child feeding;
- optimal use of parental (or other) resources to protect from infection and care for the sick child, or other vulnerable members of society (e.g. the disabled, elderly).

More generally it includes nurturing the full psychological and emotional well-being, which are goals in themselves, and which in turn may benefit nutrition and health. (ACC/SCN 1991:14)

The subcommittee points out that while some of these issues are nutritional in the biological sense, many are issues of social organisation, role patterns and the division of labour in individual households. Given the increasing number of women in the paid workforce and the time pressures on working mothers, there is no reason why a nutrition policy aimed at extending the family's caring capacity should not make an effort to support mothers and reduce their burdens. In the current climate of high unemployment, there is no reason, either, why such a nutrition policy should not address the consequences of families' having unemployed members. Never mind whether they are consuming less than 33 per cent of their caloric intake as fat; what added burdens do they have, and how can they and their families be helped to cope with these burdens? Disease-based epidemiological research may not be very helpful in such an endeavour.

Concern about the diet of low-income earners currently centres on the belief that their average consumption of fat is higher than that of more affluent people. If this were found not to be the case, nutritionists would be hard pressed to justify their involvement with low-income families. In some ways, the belief that people on low incomes eat more fat than the rest of the community resembles a necessary fiction. It virtually alone justifies concern about low-income earners in Good Nutrition—despite the fact that it is based on questionable evidence.

WOMEN, FOOD AND POLITICS

Martin Pugh has described (1991) how the entry of women into British political life was tied to concerns about food. The concerns were related to Britain's dependence on imported food from colonial countries and the threat to those supplies posed by the First World War. Internal party politics and class issues such as the loss of servants from affluent homes also played a part in prompting women to go public with what had formerly been private issues. While some of the concessions won by women may have been dubious and some short-lived, Pugh comments that both the socialist and conservative sides of politics decided to satisfy some of the 'desires of women as consumers and housewives'. Yet 'the more they pursued such a strategy, the more firmly they helped entrench women in the mainstream of British political affairs' (Pugh 1991:20).

Some contemporary issues for women have a similar potential. The relationship of eating to cultural standards of female beauty is surely one of these. Just what it would take to mobilise large enough numbers of women to transform the tyranny of dieting and slimness from a private to a public issue is hard to say. However, as a starter on this road, nutrition policy and practice might emphasise the importance of women's eating more, not less food, combined with realistic opportunities for physical activity. The biological data available support this approach just as readily as they do one which encourages women to be abstemious eaters. If control of women's appearance is really control of their behaviour, this issue may have considerable emancipatory potential for women in affluent societies. The goals of nutrition policy and practice reflect the values of those who choose them. All the more reason, then, for this choice to be available to a wide spectrum of the community. Part of this process would be an appeal to a broader notion of rationality, one which extended beyond medically oriented concerns.

9

Conclusion

 Many of the cultural themes of Good Nutrition are old if not ancient, and centre on control and conservation—issues which have undeniable practical importance in terms of survival. Science-based Good Nutrition has in large part simply modernised these old beliefs. This does not imply science-based nutrition is nonsense or of no use. It is the cultural beliefs to which science is harnessed in creating Good Nutrition which need to be explored. The use of science in the diet–heart debate is authoritarian rather than authoritative, lacks an understanding of ordinary everyday lives, and, as public persuasion, resembles propaganda rather than education.

The form of Good Nutrition currently dominant in Australia, North America and Europe is seriously flawed. Its most problematic aspect is the dominance of what I have called post-swallowing expertise over the pre-swallowing domain of everyday life. Further, what was once perceived as women's food work and responsibility in the home has increasingly become the province of those interested in heart disease. This process was influenced by interests in the US attempting to gain the support of the middle class in getting 'nutrition on the agenda'. An alliance of medicine and politics in the US seems to go a long way toward explaining the uncritical adoption of the diet–heart model by medical scientists and practitioners in Australia in the late 1970s. Although many Australians see the McDonald's fast food chain as epitomising an undesirable worldwide Americanisation of food, health workers may be less inclined to accept that dietary guidance, as it is currently understood, is part of a worldwide Americanisation of Good Nutrition.

That Good Nutrition is a mixture of culture and science is perhaps obvious on reflection. But just whose culture is represented is not always so apparent. Historically, scientists have played a part in a number of reform movements related to nutrition. While it may be true that in health promotion research and evaluation, practitioners are not scientific enough and scientists not practical enough (Kok & Green 1990), in Good Nutrition, scientists may not only lack practical wisdom, they may also be unscientific. If this is so it can be attributed, at least partly, to the devaluing of those branches of knowledge that contribute to an understanding of everyday life, particularly in domestic settings. Stumbling around in an area where their expertise is alien, post-swallowing scientists have acted as missionaries rather than as scientists, just like many reformers before them.

The shift in the rationale behind Good Nutrition discussed here occurred at a time when the domestic focus of Good Nutrition was perceived, partly because of its association with women's work, as inadequate. It proved relatively easy for a high-status form of expertise to take control, at least in the discourse about eating for health. As Good Nutrition became medicalised, it moved from being largely a discussion in the domestic sphere to a medical problem linked to coronary heart disease, which led to calls for reform of the behaviour of individuals and whole populations. Good Nutrition has effectively ignored the complexities of domestic life, except for women's assumed responsibility for their own and others' food choices and heart health. In the process, it has moved nutritional understanding further from ordinary people's reach and possibly also reduced their self-confidence and feelings of control. Ironically, it was dietitians who led the way in introducing the new ideas in nutrition to Australia. The federal government did not launch its Dietary Guidelines for Australians until a year after the Australian Association of Dietitians had released its report. This may have led to an enhanced profile and stature for dietitians, but it also created a gap between them and their traditional audience, other women. From a role which predominantly informed and supported women in traditional practices, dietitians were recast in the role of reforming their sisters' behaviour. Why were dietitians not the first to point out the absence of women and their interests in the diet–heart debate? Dietitians and other (mostly female) health professionals have been recruited by the new medicalised Good Nutrition to persuade women to change both their own and others' food behaviour.

The gap between what are seen as 'ideal' ways of eating and everyday life has grown. The ideal is now predicated on a basis of reform. This gap is central to Good Nutrition, and has been promoted in public education and discussion. This has led to increased pressure on ordinary people to feel concerned about their current choices and to change their behaviour.

The commercial benefits of Good Nutrition are only too apparent in food packaging and food product advertisements. If the promise of avoiding a heart attack through dietary reform is a worthy dishonesty, the commercial world is the repository of much unworthy dishonesty, often encouraged by links to health organisations which, for a price, lend their reputation to a selected range of products. Good Nutrition has been a great commercial success.

In the early 1990s all Good Nutrition programs are underpinned by the assumption of the necessity of universal dietary reform. This assumption is made without honest reference to the likelihood of individual benefit, thus perpetuating the so-called worthy dishonesty.

An important indicator of community responses to this pressure can be seen in humorous discussions of the restrictive dietary practices associated with Good Nutrition and in the degree to which people are sceptical about and unresponsive to nutrition campaigns. Like the themes of control and conservation, this is not new. People have always rankled at being told what is good for them. It is no longer Eden's apples which destroy, but 'indulgences' at the top of the Healthy Diet Pyramid.

Program planners have yet to examine the conditions under which change in Good Nutrition comes about. Which interest groups are effective in influencing change and which issues are most likely to be the springboard for change? It is likely that there is a complex interaction of 'interests' which are promoted by their adherents with some intentional attempts at achieving particular changes (Betts 1986).

The project of reinventing Good Nutrition will recognise the importance of not separating health professionals from women in the wider community. The acceptance by female health workers in particular that they too are subject to cultural pressures to be 'good women' will help them to develop a practical and supportive rather than a reforming Good Nutrition based on the reality of women's lives and the practicalities of family living in the late twentieth century. Because of the importance of food for women in relation to their appearance and to their domestic service to men and children, this would be a huge project.

There will always be people at risk of heart disease who will benefit from advice about changing food behaviour. These people should have easy access to quality dietary advice. However, if health workers could face individuals and community groups divested of the assumed need to reform their dietary behaviour, this would open up possibilities for developing programs which creatively meet concerns arising from the world of everyday life—childcare, supermarket shopping, and other consumer food issues such as additives and understanding children's eating behaviour.

To me the one essential way in which Good Nutrition can be made less authoritarian and more a reflection of everyday life is through the renaissance of 'parochial little programs' which have no need to be part of sweeping national reform movements, programs which can be based on local needs assessments.

One final issue to be considered is what might be the negative consequences of criticising a field in which many people are energetically engaged and in which there is a lot of public interest, a field which has only recently been able to attract funds to enable more information to be made available and to encourage research and development to improve health. What are the hazards of questioning the level of optimism about health improvement made in the name of Good Nutrition in the past decade? The answer may well lie in an assessment of whether the costs of the current lack of critical assessment of 'diet–heart' views of Good Nutrition outweigh the disadvantages of creating a more sceptical climate. This book is a statement of belief that the benefit of a more sceptical climate will outweigh the costs of reduced optimism and will lead to more realistic expectations of the contribution of food to health. I hope it will make the Good Nutrition debate more inclusive in terms of who participates and free it from its problematic cultural constraints.

Bibliography

Abraham, S. & Mira, M. 1988, 'Hazards of attempted weight loss', *Medical Journal of Australia* vol. 148, pp. 324–5

Abrahams, R. 1984, 'Equal opportunity eating: A structural excursus on things of the mouth', *Ethnic and Regional Foodways in the United States. The performance of group identity*, ed. L.K. Brown & K. Mussel, University of Tennessee Press, Knoxville pp. 19–36

ACC/SCN Ad Hoc Group on Policies to Alleviate Underconsumption and Malnutrition in Deprived Areas 1991, 'Some Options for Improving Nutrition in the 1990s', *SCN News*, no. 7 (mid-1991) Supplement

Albury, R. 1983, *The Politics of Objectivity*, Deakin University Press, Geelong

Anderson, D. 1979, 'Talking with patients about their diet', *Health Education in Practice*, ed. D.C. Anderson, Croom Helm, London, pp. 177–94.

——(ed) 1986, *A Diet of Reason: Sense and Nonsense in the Healthy Eating Debate*, Social Affairs Unit, London

Aronson, N. 1982a, 'Nutrition as a social problem: A case study of entrepreneurial strategy in science', *Social Problems*, vol. 29, no. 5, pp. 474–87

——1982b, 'Social definitions of entitlement: Food needs 1885–1920', *Media, Culture and Society*, vol. 4, pp. 51–61

Atwater, W.O. 1888, 'Pecuniary economy of food', *Century Illustrated Monthly Magazine*, vol. 35, no. 3, pp. 437–46

Austin, J.E. & Hitt, C. 1979, *Nutrition Intervention in the United States: Cases and Concepts*, Ballinger, Cambridge, Mass.

Backett, K. 1990, 'Image and reality. Health enhancing behaviours in middle-class families', *Health Education Journal*, vol. 49, no. 2, pp. 61–3

Beck, U. 1992, *Risk Society*, Sage, London

Becker, M.H. 1986, 'The tyranny of health promotion', *Public Health Reviews*, vol. 14, pp. 15–25

119

Berger, P. 1974, *Pyramids of Sacrifice. Political Ethics and Social Change*, Basic Books, New York

——1989, 'Moral judgment and political action', *Dialogue*, no. 84, pp. 2–7

Better Health Commission Taskforce on Nutrition 1987, *Towards Better Nutrition for Australians*, AGPS, Canberra

Betts, K. 1986, 'The conditions of action, power and the problem of interests', *Sociological Review*, vol. 34, no. 1, pp. 39–64

Black, A.E., Ravenscroft, C. & Sims, A.J. 1984, 'The NACNE Report: Are the dietary goals realistic? Comparisons with the dietary patterns of dietitians', *Human Nutrition: Applied Nutrition*, vol. 38A, pp. 165–79

Black, A. 1987, 'Translation of dietary recommendations into food selection: a dietitian's viewpoint', *American Journal of Clinical Nutrition*, vol. 45, pp. 1399–406

Boston, A. 1993, 'What did you do in the war, mummy?', *Country Living* (UK), no. 95, November, pp 100–3

Brown, B. 1988, 'Community nutrition in Australia and the Australian Nutrition Foundation', *Journal of Food and Nutrition*, vol. 45, no. 2, pp. 46–51

Cannon, G.J. 1991, 'The history of dietary guidelines in Europe: Will the experts ever agree?', *European Journal of Clinical Nutrition*, vol. 45, Supplement 2, pp. 54–6

Caplan, P. 1988, 'Engendering knowledge. The politics of ethnography Part 1', *Anthropology Today*, vol. 4, no. 6, pp. 8–12

Carmelli, D., Swan, G.E. & Rosenman, R.H. 1985, 'The relationship between wives' social and psychological status and their husbands' coronary heart disease. A case-control family study from the Western Collaborative Group', *American Journal of Epidemiology*, vol. 122, no. 1, pp. 90–100

Carpenter, K.J. 1994, 'The life and times of W.O. Atwater (1844–1907)', *Journal of Nutrition*, vol. 124, no. 9S, pp. 1707S–14S

Carr, W. & Kemmis, S. 1986, *Becoming Critical: Education Knowledge and Action Research*, Deakin University Press, Geelong

Chalmers, A.F. 1982, *What Is This Thing Called Science?*, 2nd edn, University of Queensland Press, St Lucia

Chapman, S. 1990, 'Intersectoral action to improve nutrition: the roles of the state and private sector. A case study from Australia', *Health Promotion International*, vol. 5, no. 1, pp. 35–44

Charles, N. & Kerr, M. 1986, 'Issues in the responsibility and control in the feeding of families', *The Politics of Health Education: Raising the Issues*, eds. Sue Rodmell & Alison Watts, Routledge & Kegan Paul, London

Clements, F.W. 1986, *A History of Human Nutrition in Australia*, Longman Cheshire, Melbourne

Cole-Hamilton, I., Gunner, K., Leverkus, C., & Starr, J. 1986, 'A study among dietitians and adult members of their households of the practicalities and implications of following proposed dietary guidelines for the UK', *Human Nutrition: Applied Nutrition*, vol. 40A, pp. 365–89

Commonwealth Department of Health Housing and Community Services. 1992, *National Nutrition Policy*, AGPS, Canberra

Cook, P. 1991, *The Independent Monthly* (Australia), August, p. 15

Cotton, P. 1990, 'Is there still too much extrapolation from data on middle-aged white men?', *Journal of the American Medical Association*, vol. 263, no. 8, pp. 1049–50, 1055

Counihan, C. 1988, 'Female identity, food and power in contemporary Florence', *Anthropological Quarterly*, vol. 61, no. 2, pp. 51–62

Crawford, D.A. & Worsley, A. 1988, 'Dieting and slimming practices of South Australian women', *Medical Journal of Australia*, vol. 148, pp. 325–31

Crotty, P. 1988, 'The disabled in institutions. Transforming functional into domestic modes of food provision', *Food Habits in Australia. The First Deakin/Sydney Universities Symposium on Australian Nutrition*, eds A.S. Truswell & M.L. Wahlqvist, Renee Gordon, North Balwyn

Crouse, J.R. 1990, 'Gender, lipoproteins, diet, and cardiovascular risk. Sauce for the goose may not be sauce for the gander', *Lancet*, vol. 1, pp. 318–20

CSIRO 1993, *The Australian Food Survey 1993. The Summary*, CSIRO Department of Human Nutrition, Adelaide

Davies, J. 1987, *The Wartime Kitchen and Garden: The Home Front 1939–45*, BBC Books, London

Davis, A.M. 1987, 'Heart health campaigns. The basis for action', *Health Education Journal*, vol. 46, no. 1, pp. 3–10

Davison, C., Davey Smith, G. & Frankel, S. 1991, 'Lay epidemiology and the prevention paradox: The implications of coronary candidacy for health education', *Sociology of Health and Illness*, vol. 13, no. 1, pp. 1–19

Day, H.G. 1987, 'E.V. McCollum and public understanding of foods and nutrition', *Nutrition Today*, vol. 22, no. 3, pp. 31–9

Doyal, L. 1979, *The Political Economy of Health*, Pluto Press, London.

Eaker, E.D., Haynes, S.G. & Feinlab, M. 1983, 'Spouse behaviour and coronary heart disease in men: Prospective results from the Framingham Heart Study ll. Modification of risk in Type A husbands according to the social and psychological status of their wives', *American Journal of Epidemiology*, vol. 118, no. 1, pp. 23–41

Easterbrook, P. J., Berlin, J.A., Gopalan, R. & Mathews, D.R. 1991, 'Publication bias in clinical research', *Lancet*, vol. 337, no. 8746, pp. 867–72

Edema, J.M.P. 1991 (Book Review), '*Nutrition Policy for Food-Rich*

Countries: A Strategic Analysis by N. Milio', Social Science & Medicine, vol. 32, no. 12, p. 1437

Ehrenreich, B. & English, D. 1973, Complaints and Disorders: The Sexual Politics of Sickness, Feminist Press, New York

——1978, For Her Own Good 150 Years of Experts Advice to Women, Anchor Press/Doubleday, New York

Ehrenreich, B. & Ehrenreich, J. 1978, 'Medicine and social control', The Cultural Crisis of Modern Medicine, ed. J. Ehrenreich, Monthly Review Press, New York

Englehardt, quoted in Walden, 'The road to Fat City', p. 367

Farquhar, J.W., Fortmann, S.P., Flora, J.A. et al. 1990, 'Effects of communitywide education on cardiovascular disease risk factors. The Stanford Five-City project', Journal of the American Medical Association, vol. 264, no. 3, pp. 359–65

Field, J.O. 1983, 'Development at the grassroots: The organisational imperative', Nutrition in the Community: A Critical Look at Nutrition Policy, Planning and Programmes, ed. D.S. McLaren, 2nd edn, Wiley, Chichester, pp. 357–71

——1985, 'Implementing nutrition programs: Lessons from an unheeded literature', Annual Review of Nutrition, vol. 5, pp. 43–72

——1987, 'Multisectoral nutrition planning: a post mortem', Food Policy, vol. 12, no.1, pp. 15–28

Fink, A. 1993, Evaluation Fundamentals. Guiding Health Programs, Research and Policies, Sage Publications, Beverly Hills

Fisher, M.F.K. 1976, 'How to Cook a Wolf', in The Art of Eating, Vintage, New York

Foreyt, J.P., Goodrick, G.K. & Gotto, A. 1981, 'Limitations of behavioural treatment of obesity. Review and analysis', Journal of Behavioural Medicine vol. 4, no. 2, pp. 159–74

Fortmann, S.P., Barr Taylor C., Flora, J.A. and Winkelby, M.A. 1993, 'Effect of community health education on plasma cholesterol levels and diet: The Stanford Five-City Project', American Journal of Epidemiology, vol. 137, no. 10, pp. 1039–55

Frankel, S., Davison, C. & Smith, G.D. 1991, 'Lay epidemiology and the rationality of responses to health education', British Journal of General Practice, vol. 41, pp. 428–30

Geelong Advertiser 1991, 'Chewing our own graves', 15 June, p. 7

——1991a, 'Premiers target men MPs, media', 11 March, p. 3

Gibney, M. 1990, 'Dietary guidelines: a critical appraisal', Journal of Human Nutrition and Dietetics, vol. 3, pp. 245–54.

Glanz, K. 1990, 'The cholesterol controversy and health education: A response to the critics', Patient Education and Counselling, vol. 16, pp. 89–90

Goble, A. 1989, 'Do caring wives protect against cardiac disease?', Medical Journal of Australia, vol. 151, pp. 183–4

Goode, J.G., Curtis, K. & Theophano, J. 1984, 'Menu formats, meal cycles, and menu negotiation in the maintenance of an Italian-American community', *Food in the Social Order. Studies of Food and Festivities in Three American Communities*, ed. Mary Douglas, Russel Sage Foundation, New York

Grundy, S. 1990, 'Cholesterol and coronary heary disease. Future directions', *Journal of the American Medical Association*, vol. 264, no. 23, pp. 3053–9

Gussow, J.D. & Clancy, K.L. 1986, 'Dietary guidelines for sustainability', *Journal of Nutrition Education*, vol. 18, no. 1, pp. 1–5

Guthrie, H.A. 1987, 'Principles and issues in translating dietary recomendations to food selection: a nutrition educator's point of view', *American Journal of Clinical Nutrition*, vol. 45, pp. 1394–8

Harvey, P.W.J., Marks, G.C., Bain, C. & Heywood, P.F. 1990, 'Are dietary goals and guidelines enough?', *Medical Journal of Australia*, vol. 153, pp. 442–3

Haynes, S.G., Eaker, E.D. & Feinlab, M. 1983, 'Spouse behaviour and coronary heart disease in men: Prospective results from the Framingham Heart Study 1. Concordance of risk factors and the relationship of psychosocial status to coronary incidence', *American Journal of Epidemiology*, vol. 118, no. 1, pp. 1–21

Health 84, 1984, no. 19, June, p. 1

Health Targets and Implementation Committee 1990, *Health for All Australians*, AGPS, Canberra

Hegsted, D.M. 1990, 'Recollections of pioneers in nutrition; fifty years in nutrition, *Journal of the American College of Nutrition*, vol. 9, no. 4, pp. 280–7

——quoted in Austin & Hitt, *Nutrition Intervention*, p. 339

Hertzler, A.A. & Anderson, H.L. 1974, 'Food guides in the United States', *Journal of the American Dietetic Association*, vol. 64, pp. 19–28

Heywood, P. & Lund-Adams, M. 1991, 'The Australian food and nutrition system: a basis for policy formulation and analysis', *Australian Journal of Public Health*, vol. 15, no. 4, pp. 258–70

James, A. 1979, 'Conceptions, concoctions and confections', *Journal of the Anthropological Society of Oxford*, vol. 10, no. 2, pp. 83–95

Johnstone, J.R. & Ulyatt, C., 1991, 'Health scare: The misuse of science in public health policy', *Critical Issues no. 14*, Australian Institute for Public Policy, Perth

Journal of the American Dietetic Association 1942, 'National industrial nutrition program', vol. 18, p. 596

——1942a, 'Nutrition for housewives', vol. 18, pp. 756–7

——1943, 'A victory lunch', vol. 19, p. 129

Katroulis, G. 1990, 'The orifice revisited: Women in gynaecological texts', *Community Health Studies*, vol. 14, no. 1. pp. 73–84

Kendler, H.H. 1993, 'Psychology and the ethics of social policy', *American Psychologist,* vol. 48, no. 19, pp. 1046–53

Keys, A. 1968. 'Official collective recommendation on diet in the Scandinavian countries', *Nutrition Reviews*, vol. 26, no. 9, pp. 259–63

——1990, 'Recollections of pioneers in nutrition: from starvation to cholesterol, *Journal of the American College of Nutrition*, vol. 9, no. 4, pp. 288-91

Kimmel, A.J. 1991, 'Predictable biases in the ethical decision making of American psychologists', *American Psychologist*, vol. 46, no. 7, pp. 786–8

Kok, G. & Green, L.W. 1990, 'Research to support health promotion in practice: A plea for increased co-operation', *Health Promotion International*, vol. 5, no. 4 pp. 303–8

Koren, C. & Klein, N. 1991, 'Bias against negative studies in newspaper reports of medical research, *Journal of the American Medical Association*, vol. 266, no. 13, pp. 1824–6

Lee, S. H. 1988, *Women's Health Data Requirements*, AGPS, Canberra

Leupker, R.V., Murray, D.M., Jacobs, D.R., Mittelmark, M.B., *et al.* 1994, 'Community education for cardiovascular disease prevention: risk factor changes in the Minnesota Heart Health Program', *American Journal of Public Health*, vol. 84, no. 9, pp. 1383–93

Levenstein, H.A. 1988, *Revolution at the Table: The Transformation of the American Diet*, Oxford University Press, New York

——1993, *Paradox of Plenty: A Social History of Eating in America*, Oxford University Press, New York

Malcolm, J.A. & Dobson, A.J. 1989, 'Marriage is associated with a lower risk of heart disease in men', *Medical Journal of Australia*, vol. 151, pp. 185–8

Marantz, P. R. 1990, 'Blaming the victim: The negative consequences of preventive medicine, *American Journal of Public Health*, vol. 80, no. 10, pp. 1186–7

Mathews, K.A., Kelsey, S.F., Meilahn, E.N., *et al.* 1989, 'Educational attainment and behavioral and biological risk factors for coronary heart disease in middle-aged women', *American Journal of Epidemiology*, vol. 129, no. 6, pp. 1132–44

Mayer, J. 1990, 'Nutritional problems in the United States: Then and now two decades later', *Nutrition Today*, vol. 25, no. 1, pp. 15–19

McCormick, J. & Skrabanek, P. 1988, 'Coronary heart disease is not preventable by population interventions', *Lancet*, vol. 2, pp. 839–41

McGovern, G. 1975, *Congressional Record Proceedings and Debates of the 94th Congress, First Session, Washington Monday June 16 1975*, vol. 121, no. 94

McIntosh, W.A. & Zey, M. 1989, 'Women as gatekeepers of food consumption: A sociological critique', *Food and Foodways*, vol. 3, no. 4, pp. 317–22

McLaughlin, T. 1978, *A Diet of Tripe: The chequered history of food reform*, Newton Abbot, London

Mead, M. 1943, 'The factor of food habits', *Journal of the American Dietetic Association*, vol. 19, p. 189

Milio, N. 1990, *Nutrition Policy for Food Rich Countries. A Strategic Analysis*, Johns Hopkins University Press, Baltimore

Miller, M., Swanson, M., Coli, T., *et al.* 1987, 'Facts on fat: A community nutrition education campaign', *Journal of Food and Nutrition*, vol. 44, no. 2, pp. 61–5

Miller, S.A. & Stephenson, M.G. 1985, 'Scientific and public health rationale for the dietary guidelines for Americans', *American Journal of Clinical Nutrition*, vol. 42, pp. 739–45

Moore, T.J. 1989, *Heart Failure: A Critical Inquiry into American Medicine and the Revolution in Health Care*, Random House, New York

Nader, L. 1984, 'Up the anthropologist—perspectives gained from studying up' *Anthropology for the Nineties. Introductory Readings*, ed. J.B. Cole, Free Press, New York, pp. 470–84

National Health and Medical Research Council 1989, *Implementing the Dietary Guidelines for Australians: Report of the Subcommittee on Nutrition Education*, AGPS, Canberra

Nestel, P. 1989, 'Dietary guidelines—USA looks again', *Food Australia*, vol. 41, no. 8, pp. 888–9

Nestle, M. 1990, 'National nutrition monitoring policy. The continuing need for legislative intervention', *Journal of Nutrition Education*, vol. 22, no. 3, pp. 141–4

O'Dea, J.A. 1991, 'Trends in the nutrition and health status of Australians. Are we creating adverse effects?', *Journal of the Home Economics Association*, vol. 23, no. 2, pp. 57–61

Orbach, S. 1978, *Fat is a Feminist Issue*, Berkeley Publishing, New York

Pelto, G.H., Pelto, P.J. & Messer, E. (eds) 1989, *Research Methods in Nutritional Anthropology*, United Nations University, Tokyo

Popkin, B., Haines, P.S. & Reidy, K.C. 1989, 'Food consumption trends of US women: patterns and determinants between 1977 and 1985', *American Journal of Clinical Nutrition*, vol. 49, pp. 1307–19

Priestland, G. 1972, *Frying Tonight: The Saga of Fish and Chips*, Gentry Books, London

Probert, C.S.J., Maddison, W., Roland, J.M. 1990, 'Diet, diabetes and male chauvinism', *British Medical Journal*, vol. 310, pp. 1430–1

Pugh, M. 1991, 'Women, food and politics, 1880–1920', *History Today*, vol. 41, March, pp. 14–20

Puska, P., Aulikki, N., Tuomilehto, N., *et al.* 1985, 'The community-based strategy to prevent coronary heart disease: Conclusions from the ten years of the North Karelia Project', *Annual Review of Public Health*, vol. 6, pp. 147–93

Rifkin, S.B. & Walt, G. 1986, 'Why health improves: Defining the issues concerning "comprehensive primary health care" and "selective primary health care" ', *Social Science & Medicine*, vol. 23, pp. 559–66

Risk Factor Prevalence Study Management Committee 1990, *Risk Factor Prevalence Study: Survey Number 3 1989*, National Heart Foundation of Australia and Australian Institute of Health and Welfare, Canberra

Ritzer, G. 1993, *The McDonaldisation of Society*, Sage, London

Rivers, J.P.W. 1979, 'The profession of nutrition—an historical perspective', *Proceedings of the Nutrition Society*, vol. 38, pp. 225–31

Rodmell, S. & Watts, A. (eds.) 1986, *The Politics of Health Education: Raising the Issues*, Routledge & Kegan Paul, London

Rose, G. 1985, 'Sick individuals and sick populations', *International Journal of Epidemiology*, vol. 14, no. 1, pp. 32–8

Rosen, G. 1974, 'Ellen H. Richards (1842–1911): Sanitary chemist and pioneer of professional equality for women in health science', *American Journal of Public Health*, vol. 64, no. 8, pp. 816–19

Salonen, J.T. 1987, 'Did the North Karelia Project reduce coronary mortality?', *Lancet*, vol. 2, p. 269

Scambler, G. 1987, 'Habermas and the power of medical expertise' in *Sociological Theory and Medical Sociology*, ed. G. Scambler, Tavistock Publications, London, pp. 165–93

Schwartz, H. 1986, *Never Satisfied. A Cultural History of Diets, Fantasies and Fat*, Free Press, New York

Scrimshaw, N.S. & Gleason, G.R. (eds.) 1992, *Rapid Assessment Procedures: Qualitative Methodologies for Planning and Evaluation of Health Related Programs*, International Foundation for Developing Countries, Boston

Scrimshaw, S. & Hurtado, E. 1987, *Rapid Assessment Procedures for Nutrition and Primary Health Care: Anthropological Approaches to Improving Programme Effectiveness*, United Nations University, Tokyo, and UCLA Latin American Center Publications, Los Angeles

Sherraden, M.S. 1991, 'Policy impacts of community participation: Health services in rural Mexico', *Human Organization*, vol. 50, no. 3, pp. 256–63

Skrabanek, P. 1990, 'Nonsensus consensus', *Lancet*, vol. 335, pp. 1446–7

Spitzer, L. & Rodin, J. 1981, 'Human eating behaviour: a critical review of studies in normal weight and overweight individuals', *Appetite*, vol. 2, pp. 293–329

Stanton Hicks, C. 1972, *Who Called the Cook a Bastard?: A Personal Account of a One-Man Campaign to Improve the Feeding of the Soldier*, Keyline Publications, Sydney

Stone, D. 1991, 'Recession may be causing waist inflation', *Sunday Age*, Melbourne, 24 March

Strogatz, D.S., Siscovick, D.S., Weiss, N.S. & Rennart, G. 1988, 'Wife's level of education and husband's risk of primary cardiac arrest', *American Journal of Public Health*, vol. 18, no. 11, pp. 1491–3

Suarez, L. & Barret-Connor, E. 1984, 'Is an educated wife hazardous to your health?', *American Journal of Epidemiology*, vol. 119, no. 2, pp. 244–9

——1985, (letter) 'The authors reply', *American Journal of Epidemiology*, vol. 122, no.1, pp. 193–4

Tolisson, B. 1993, 'Nutrition campaign makes an impact', *Meat and Livestock Review*, August, pp. 14–15

Truswell, A.S. 1983, 'The development of dietary guidelines', *Food Technology in Australia*, vol. 35, no. 11, pp. 498–502

——1987, 'Evolution of dietary recommendations, goals and guidelines', *American Journal of Clinical Nutrition*, vol. 45, no. 5, pp. 1060–72

Turner, B.S. 1982, 'The government of the body: Medical regimens and the rationalization of diet', *British Journal of Sociology*, vol. 33, no. 2, pp. 254–69

van Manen, M. 1990, *Researching Lived Experience: Human Science for an Action Sensitive Pedagogy*, State University of New York Press, Albany

Veatch, R. 1991, 'Consensus of expertise: The role of consensus of experts in formulating public policy and estimating facts', *Journal of Medicine and Philosophy*, vol. 16, no. 4, pp. 427–45

Veatch, R.M. & Moreno, J.D. 1991, 'Consensus in panels and committees: conceptual and ethical issues', *Journal of Medicine and Philosophy*, vol. 16, no. 4, pp. 371–3

Vincenti, V. 1987, 'Science and sexism: The historical influence on home economics today', *Journal of Home Economics*, vol. 79, no. 4. pp. 45–9

Walden, K, 1985, 'The road to Fat City: An interpretation of the development of weight consciousness in Western society', *Historical Reflections*, vol. 12, no. 3, pp. 331–73

Walker, R. & Roberts, D. 1988, *From Scarcity to Surfeit. A History of Food and Nutrition in New South Wales*, University of New South Wales Press, Sydney

Walton, J.K. 1989, 'Fish and chips and the British working class, 1870–1930', *Journal of Social History*, vol. 23, no. 2, pp. 243–66

Waring, M. 1988, *Counting for Nothing: What Men Value and What Women are Worth*, Allen & Unwin, Sydney

Widdowson, E. 1987, 'Atwater: A personal tribute from the United Kingdom', *American Journal of Clinical Nutrition*, vol. 45, pp. 898–904

Wolf, N. 1990, *The Beauty Myth*, Chatto & Windus, New York

Worsley, A. 1991, 'Food policy and nutrition promotion', *Food Australia*, vol. 43, no. 2, pp. 540–7

Worsley, A. & Worsley. A. 1988, 'The performance of domestic tasks—a survey of South Australian women', *Journal of the Home Economics Association of Australia*, vol. 21, pp. 37–9

Zebich, M. 1979, *The Politics of Nutrition: Issue Definition, Agenda-Setting and Policy Formulation in the United States*, PhD Thesis, University of New Mexico, Albuquerque

Zola, I.K. 1972, 'Medicine as an institution of social control' *Sociological Review*, vol. 20, no. 4, pp. 487–504

Index